Cryptocurrency for Seniors

Maximilian Natal

CONTENTS

Chapter One

The year 2020 was the first time in human history when there were more retirees than births. Industrialized countries across the globe are experiencing a significant demographic shift characterized by an aging population. There will be implications for healthcare systems, labor markets, social welfare, and, above all else, economics. As a society gets older, its purchasing habits change. People buy fewer consumer goods (like houses, cars and washing machines) and money flows more towards services (such as vacations and healthcare). Some economists refer to this as The Silver Economy.

This book sets out to explain how you can handle your own silver with better effectiveness vis-à-vis cryptocurrency.

Defining Cryptocurrency and its Relevance in Today's Digital World

In today's rapidly evolving digital landscape, cryptocur-rency has emerged as a revolutionary concept that has gained immense popularity and disrupted traditional financial systems. "Cryptocurrency" refers to digital or virtual currencies that employ cryptographic techniques to secure transactions, control the creation of new units, and verify the transfer of assets.

The concept of using cryptography to secure

transactions and preserve privacy dates back to the 1970s. Cypherpunks, a group of computer scientists and activists, emerged in the 1980s, advocating for the use of cryptography as a means to protect civil liberties, including financial privacy.

In the early 1990s, David Chaum developed DigiCash, an electronic cash system that incorporated cryptographic techniques for secure transactions. Although DigiCash faced challenges and eventually ceased operations, it laid the groundwork for future developments in digital currencies.

Fast-forward to 2008 when an anonymous individual (or group operating under the pseudonym "Satoshi Nakamoto") published the Bitcoin whitepaper, titled *Bitcoin: A Peer-to-Peer Electronic Cash System*. This marked the birth of Bitcoin, the first decentralized cryptocurrency.

Nakamoto's whitepaper introduced the concept of blockchain, a distributed ledger that records all Bitcoin transactions. This technology enabled the decentralized verification and security of transactions without the need for intermediaries.

On January 3, 2009, Nakamoto mined the first block of the Bitcoin blockchain, known as the "Genesis Block." This event marked the official launch of Bitcoin, and it included a message referencing a headline from *The Times* newspaper, emphasizing the system's timestamp and its departure from traditional financial institutions.

Bitcoin gradually gained traction among technologists, libertarians, and early adopters, who recognized its potential as a decentralized digital currency. Mining communities and online forums dedicated to Bitcoin flourished, contributing to its growth. As the cryptocurrency ecosystem expanded, alternative cryptocurrencies, known as altcoins, began to emerge. Litecoin, created by Charlie Lee in 2011, aimed to offer faster transaction confirmations compared to Bitcoin. Other notable altcoins include Namecoin, Ripple, and Ethereum, each with its unique features and objectives.

Over time, cryptocurrency gained recognition as a legitimate asset class, attracting attention from investors, financial institutions, and governments. Major companies and organizations, including Microsoft, PayPal, and Tesla, started accepting Bitcoin as a form of payment.

Governments worldwide have responded to the rise of cryptocurrencies by developing regulatory frameworks. Some countries, like Japan, embraced cryptocurrencies, while others introduced regulations to address concerns such as money-laundering and consumer protection.

ICOs (Initial Coin Offerings) emerged as a popular crowdfunding method, allowing projects to raise funds by issuing and selling tokens on blockchain platforms. ICOs provided an avenue for startups to secure capital and attracted significant investment, but they also faced regulatory scrutiny due to potential fraud and lack of investor protection.

The underlying blockchain technology gained attention for its potential beyond cryptocurrencies.

Industries such as finance, supply chain management, healthcare, and voting systems explored blockchain applications, with projects like Ethereum offering programmable smart contracts and decentralized applications (dApps).

Not everything about cryptocurrencies is rosy, though. They've been known for their price volatility and face challenges in achieving stability and mainstream acceptance. As cryptocurrencies gained popularity, moreover, scalability became a pressing concern. Bitcoin's network, for instance, faced limitations in transaction-speed. Additionally, the energy-consump-tion associated with mining has raised environmental concerns, driving the need for more sustainable solutions.

Nevertheless, governments and central banks worldwide have started exploring the development of Central Bank Digital Currencies. CBDCs aim to combine the benefits of cryptocurrencies, such as efficiency and security, with the control and stability provided by central authorities.

But before we address those issues, let's return to the basics. . . .

I. Cryptocurrency Fundamentals

Cryptocurrencies, such as Bitcoin, Ethereum, and Litecoin, are (just to reiterate) decentralized systems that rely on blockchain technology to operate. Blockchain, a distributed ledger that records all transactions across a network of computers, ensures transparency, security, and immutability.

CRYPTOCURRENCY FOR SENIORS

In the realm of traditional banking (before Blockchain), banks essentially provided three main functions: firstly, offering a repository for cash; secondly, extending loans; and, thirdly, giving depositors a ledger of accounts.

These ledgers played a vital role in ensuring the accurate recording, tracking, and management of financial transactions. Originally, ledgers were physical books where accountants manually entered and maintained records. However, with the advent of digital technologies, ledgers have evolved into electronic systems that enhance efficiency, security, and accessibility. They provide certain functions, such as:

1. Record Keeping: Ledgers served as a comprehensive repository for recording and organizing financial transactions. They provided a chronological and systematic account of all inflows and outflows of funds within a banking institution. This record-keeping function is essential for maintaining transparency, tracking balances, and facilitating audits or regulatory compliance.

2. Account Management: Ledgers enable banks to manage customer accounts effectively. Each customer has an individual ledger that tracks their deposits, withdrawals, interest earned, fees charged, and other relevant information. This information helps banks provide accurate statements to customers,

facilitate transactions, and address customer inquiries or disputes.

3. Balance Calculation: Ledgers play a critical role in calculating and maintaining accurate balances for each customer account. By recording deposits and withdrawals, ledgers track the available balance in an account, allowing customers and banks to monitor account status in real-time. This information is crucial for ensuring sufficient funds for transactions and avoiding overdrafts or other account-related issues.

4. Transaction Verification: Ledgers serve as a means to verify the authenticity and integrity of financial transactions. By recording each transaction, including the parties involved, amounts, dates, and any accompanying documentation, ledgers provide an audit trail that can be reviewed and verified. This function enhances accountability, reduces the risk of fraud or errors, and enables banks to investigate any discrepancies.

5. Reporting and Analysis: Ledgers provide the foundation for generating various reports and conducting financial analysis. By consolidating transactional data, ledgers enable banks to prepare financial statements, such as balance sheets, income statements, and cash flow statements. These reports offer insights into the bank's financial health, performance, and trends, aiding decision-

making, risk assessment, and strategic planning.

6. Regulatory Compliance: Ledgers play a crucial role in ensuring compliance with regulatory requirements. Banks must maintain accurate and complete records of financial transactions to adhere to anti-money laundering (AML) regulations, know-your-customer (KYC) guidelines, and other regulatory frameworks. Ledgers enable banks to track and report suspicious activities, monitor transaction patterns, and provide necessary information during audits or regulatory examinations.

At any rate, Blockchain offers a new sort of digital ledger. The only difference is that it cuts out the bank as a middle-man.

Unlike traditional currencies controlled by central banks, cryptocurrencies are typically not issued or regulated by any centralized authority. This decentralized nature eliminates intermediaries, reduces transaction costs, and enhances financial inclusion.

II. Key Features of Cryptocurrency

Security and Privacy: Cryptocurrencies employ cryptographic algorithms to secure transactions and protect users' identities. The use of public and private keys ensures that transactions are secure, traceable, and resistant to fraud or hacking attempts.

Decentralization: The absence of a central authority

in cryptocurrency systems prevents any single entity from controlling or manipulating the currency. Decentralization fosters trust, eliminates the risk of corruption, and empowers individuals to have greater control over their financial assets.

Transparency: Blockchain technology allows for transparent and publicly auditable transactions. Every transaction is recorded on a distributed ledger, providing an immutable history of all activities. This transparency enhances accountability and trust within the cryptocurrency ecosystem.

III. Relevance of Cryptocurrency in the Digital World

Cryptocurrencies have the potential to provide financial services to the unbanked and underbanked populations worldwide. With only a smartphone and internet access, individuals can participate in the global economy, send and receive funds, and access financial services without the need for a traditional bank account.

Cryptocurrencies enable seamless cross-border transactions without the need for intermediaries, such as financial institutions or payment processors. This capability simplifies and accelerates international trade, removes currency conversion barriers, and reduces transaction costs.

Cryptocurrencies facilitate direct peer-to-peer transactions, eliminating the need for intermediaries and reducing associated fees. This enables individuals to transact directly with one another, empowering decentralized commerce and removing barriers to entry for entrepreneurs and small businesses.

The advent of cryptocurrencies has sparked many new innovations. Smart contracts, decentralized applications, and non-fungible tokens (NFTs) are just a few examples of the inventive applications enabled by cryptocurrencies.

IV. Challenges and Future Outlook

Cryptocurrencies are known for their price volatility, which poses risks to investors and mainstream adoption. Additionally, regulatory frameworks around the world are still evolving, creating uncertainty and concerns about illicit activities, money laundering, and tax evasion. Striking a balance between innovation and regulation remains a significant challenge.

As cryptocurrencies gain popularity, scalability also becomes a crucial concern. Bitcoin's network, for instance, faces limitations in terms of transaction speed and adaptability. Cryptocurrencies are still in the early stages of development, and their evolution is ongoing. Integration with existing financial systems, cooperation with regulatory bodies, and addressing scalability and energy consumption concerns are key to their continued relevance and expanding horizons.

The upshot is that cryptocurrency represents a paradigm shift in the way we perceive and interact with money and financial systems. Its relevance in today's digital world cannot be understated, as it offers enhanced security, privacy, financial inclusion, and the potential for disruptive innovation. While challenges remain, the evolution and integration of cryptocurrencies hold promise for reshaping our financial landscape and fostering a more inclusive and decentralized global economy. As cryptocurrencies continue to evolve, it is crucial for stakeholders to collaborate, innovate, and address concerns to unlock their full potential.

Understanding the Basics of Blockchain Technology

To understand the structure of Blockchain, one has to understand that (just as the name suggests) it consists of a chain of "blocks," each containing a set of transactions. These blocks are linked together using cryptographic hashes, forming an immutable and tamper-evident ledger.

"Hashes" are unique identifiers. Hash functions convert input data of any size into fixed-length alphanumeric strings. The output, known as the hash, is unique to the input data. Hashing ensures the integrity and security of data within the blockchain.

Blockchain relies on cryptographic algorithms for secure and private transactions. Public-key cryptography, which utilizes pairs of public and private keys, enables participants to verify transactions and ensure data authenticity.

Unlike centralized systems, blockchain operates on a peer-to-peer network, where multiple nodes validate and maintain the ledger. This decentralized structure eliminates the need for intermediaries and enhances transparency and trust.

CRYPTOCURRENCY FOR SENIORS

I. How Blockchain Works

When a transaction occurs, it is broadcast to the network. Nodes known as miners collect these transactions and validate their authenticity using consensus mechanisms, such as Proof of Work (PoW) or Proof of Stake (PoS).

Consensus mechanisms are procedures for ensuring agreement among network participants about the validity of transactions. PoW requires miners to solve complex mathematical puzzles, while PoS relies on validators who hold a stake in the network. Consensus mechanisms prevent double-spending and maintain the integrity of the blockchain.

Once a set of transactions is validated, miners bundle them into a block. The miner who successfully solves the puzzle or the validator chosen through PoS adds the block to the blockchain, linking it to the previous block through the hash. This process creates a fixed and tamper-proof chain of blocks.

Blockchain achieves security through cryptographic techniques, decentralization, and consensus mechanisms. As each block contains a hash that references the previous block, altering a single block would require changing the entire chain, making it computationally infeasible and ensuring the tamper-evident nature of the ledger.

II. Potential Applications of Blockchain Technology

Even though Blockchain is associated in the popular imagination with aforementioned cryprocurrencies like Bitcoin or Ethereum, it's also attractive to logistics experts who like its offer of traceability and transparency for use in supply chains, where it can be used to record the movement of goods and verify their authenticity. This helps prevent counterfeiting, enhances efficiency, and promotes ethical sourcing.

Blockchain also has the potential to streamline and transform traditional financial systems. It can facilitate faster, cheaper, and more secure cross-border payments, enable smart contracts for automated transactions, and provide financial services to people who can't get bank accounts.

In addition, Blockchain has practical applications in the medical field, whereby it can enhance the security and interoperability of medical records, ensuring privacy, reducing fraud, and enabling seamless sharing of patient data across healthcare providers. It also has applications in clinical trials and telemedicine.

Moreover, Blockchain offers a decentralized and secure approach to identity management. It enables individuals to have control over their personal information, simplifies identity verification processes, and reduces the risk of data-breaches or identity theft.

III. Challenges and Future Outlook

Blockchain faces scalability challenges, particularly in public networks, due to the computational requirements of consensus mechanisms. Efforts are underway to improve scalability through techniques like sharding, layer-2 solutions, and alternative consensus algorithms.

There are other challenges, too. For instance, as blockchain networks proliferate, achieving interoperability between different blockchains becomes crucial for seamless data exchange and collaboration. Standards and protocols are being developed to facilitate interoperability across various blockchain platforms.

Blockchain's decentralized nature poses challenges in terms of regulatory frameworks and legal implications. Governments worldwide are developing regulations to address concerns related to privacy, data protection, financial transactions, and smart contracts.

The future of blockchain technology lies in ongoing research and development. Advancements in areas such as privacy, scalability, energy efficiency, and user experience will drive the adoption and evolution of blockchain applications.

To recap: Blockchain technology has emerged as a disruptive force with immense potential across various sectors. By leveraging decentralized networks, cryptography, and consensus mechanisms, blockchain offers transparency, security, and efficiency. Understanding the basics of blockchain technology, from its structure and components to its applications, is crucial in harnessing its transformative power. While challenges exist, ongoing research and innovation will drive the evolution of blockchain, shaping the future of finance, supply chain management, healthcare, and many other industries.

CRYPTOCURRENCY FOR SENIORS

Exploring the Benefits and Potential Risks of Cryptocurrency for Seniors

While often associated with younger generations, cryptocurrency presents unique opportunities for seniors. One important factor is that it offers a measure of financial inclusion and independence.

Financial independence plays a crucial role in the lives of older people (our single fastest-growing demographic), providing them with security, dignity, and the ability to enjoy their retirement years. Being in control of their own economic destiny allows senior citizens to rely on their own savings and investments rather than being dependent solely on government assistance or family-support. Having a solid financial foundation provides peace-of-mind and a sense of security during retirement.

Financial independence, moreover, enables seniors to navigate unexpected expenses, such as medical emergencies or home repairs, without compromising their well-being or burdening their loved ones. It empowers them to handle unforeseen circumstances with confidence and resilience.

Seniors who are financially independent are less vulnerable to financial abuse or exploitation by unscrupulous individuals or organizations. They can make informed decisions about their finances and protect their assets, ensuring their financial well-being and autonomy.

Furthermore, financial independence allows senior citizens to access quality healthcare services without restrictions. They can afford necessary medical treatments, medications, and regular check-ups, prioritizing their health and well-being. It also enables them to explore various long-term care options, including home healthcare, assisted living facilities, or nursing homes, based on their preferences and needs. They can maintain control over their living-arrangements and receive the medical attention they require, enhancing their overall quality of life.

Additionally, financial independence provides seniors with the opportunity to plan and prepare for their future long-term care needs. This relieves the burden on their family members, who can have peace-of-mind knowing that their loved ones' care is adequately financed.

Having that freedom also allows senior citizens to make choices that align with their preferred lifestyle. They can pursue hobbies, travel, engage in social activities, and enjoy their retirement years without financial constraints. This, needless to say, is great for emotional well-being, which fosters better health outcomes.

Likewise, financial independence gives senior citizens the ability to provide support to their children, grandchildren, or other family members if needed. It allows them to contribute to family milestones, celebrations, and provide assistance during times of financial hardship.

With financial independence, seniors have the option to age in place, remaining in their homes and communities for as long as possible. They can invest in necessary modifications to make their homes safe and comfortable, ensuring independence and a sense of familiarity. It empowers seniors to make decisions that correspond with their values and priorities. They can choose *how* to spend their money, support causes they care about, and engage in activities that bring them joy and fulfillment.

Being in control of their own finances allows older men and women to maintain control over their own lives and keeps them mentally sharp. They can manage their resources, budget effectively, and plan for future needs, maintaining their sense of autonomy and self-sufficiency.

Financial independence also enables seniors to plan their legacy, ensuring that their assets are distributed according to their wishes. They can make arrangements for estate planning, philanthropy, or providing for future generations, leaving a meaningful impact on their loved ones and society.

Some of the ways that cryptocurrencies can help seniors achieve all this is by means of the following:

A. Access to Financial Services: Cryptocurrency can provide seniors with access to financial services, especially those who have limited access to traditional banking infrastructure. By using a smartphone or computer, seniors can participate in the global economy, send and receive funds, and store wealth independently.

B. Inflation Hedge: Cryptocurrencies like Bitcoin have a limited supply and are not subject to inflation caused by central banks. This characteristic makes them potentially attractive to seniors seeking to preserve the value of their wealth and mitigate the impact of rising costs.

C. Remittances: For seniors living in different countries or relying on financial support from family members abroad, cryptocurrency can offer a cost-effective and faster alternative to traditional remittance services. It eliminates intermediaries, reduces fees, and provides quicker cross-border transactions.

In addition, cyptocurrency provides an opportunity for seniors to diversify their investment portfolios beyond traditional asset classes like stocks and bonds. By including cryptocurrencies, seniors may potentially benefit from the growth and returns associated with this emerging asset class.

Cryptocurrency investments can be accessible to seniors with limited capital. Unlike traditional investments that may require high minimum investments, cryptocurrency allows for fractional ownership, enabling seniors to invest smaller amounts and potentially benefit from market movements.

Engaging with cryptocurrencies can offer seniors a chance to learn about new technologies, economics, and investment strategies. This continuous learning process can provide intellectual stimulation and foster a sense of curiosity and exploration.

One of the primary challenges for seniors in adopting cryptocurrency is the requirement of digital literacy and familiarity with technology. Learning to use wallets, exchanges, and other cryptocurrency platforms may present a learning curve for seniors who are less experienced with digital tools.

The decentralized nature of cryptocurrencies may expose seniors to potential risks associated with cybersecurity. Phishing attacks, scams, and malware targeting cryptocurrency holders can result in financial loss. Seniors must be vigilant, adopt best practices for online security, and exercise caution when engaging with cryptocurrency-related activities.

Simplifying user interfaces and enhancing user experiences can help overcome technological barriers. Cryptocurrency platforms that prioritize user-friendly designs and provide comprehensive support and guidance can encourage adoption among seniors.

Cryptocurrency requires secure storage to protect digital assets from theft or loss. Seniors must understand and implement protocols for securing their cryptocurrency holdings, such as using hardware wallets, enabling multi-factor authentication, and employing robust password management practices.

The evolving regulatory landscape around cryptocurrencies may present challenges for seniors seeking legal protection and oversight. Seniors should be aware of local regulations, tax implications, and potential scams associated with the cryptocurrency market.

Cryptocurrency markets are known for their volatility, with prices experiencing significant fluctuations. Seniors should consider their risk tolerance and financial goals when investing in cryptocurrencies and be prepared for potential losses.

Conclusion

Cryptocurrency offers unique benefits and potential risks for seniors. Financial inclusion, investment potential, and the opportunity to explore new technologies and investment strategies are some of the advantages that cryptocurrencies can provide. However, technological barriers, cybersecurity concerns, and the volatility of cryptocurrency markets are potential risks that seniors should consider. By understanding the risks, adopting common-sense procedures for security, and staying informed about regulatory developments, seniors can navigate the cryptocurrency landscape with prudence and make informed decisions that align with their financial goals and risk tolerance.

Chapter Two

Getting Started With Cryptocurrency

Before delving into the setup process, it is essential to grasp the concept of a digital wallet. In the world of cryptocurrencies, a digital wallet functions as a secure container to store, send, and receive digital currencies. It serves as a bridge between the user and the blockchain. Digital wallets come in various forms, such as software wallets, hardware wallets, and online wallets. Each type offers different features, security levels, and accessibility, catering to the diverse needs of users.

Regarding different types of digital wallets, one is called a software wallet. Software wallets are applications installed on electronic devices, such as computers or smartphones. They are generally categorized as either hot wallets or cold wallets. Hot wallets are connected to the internet, providing easy access for daily transactions, but may be more susceptible to security breaches. Cold wallets, on the other hand, store cryptocurrency offline, enhancing security but sacrificing convenience.

In addition, there are repositories called hardware wallets. These are physical devices specifically designed to secure cryptocurrency. They are considered one of the safest options as they store private keys offline, minimizing the risk of hacking. Hardware wallets require a connection to a computer or smartphone when performing transactions, ensuring a secure and seamless user experience.

Next, there are online wallets. Online wallets, also known as web wallets, operate through web-based platforms or exchanges. They provide convenient access to digital currencies from any internet-connected device. However, users must trust the platform's security measures and safeguard against potential hacking or phishing attacks.

The ensuing is a step-by-step process of setting up a digital wallet:

1. Research and Choose a Wallet: Thoroughly research different wallet options, considering factors such as security, ease-of-use, compatibility, and supported cryptocurrencies. Select a wallet that aligns with your specific needs and preferences.

2. Download or Access the Wallet: If you choose a software wallet, download and install the application on your device from a trusted source. For online wallets, create an account on a reputable platform, ensuring it provides robust security measures.

3. Set Up Your Wallet: Follow the instructions provided by the wallet provider to set up your wallet. This typically involves creating a strong, unique password and, in some cases, enabling additional security features such as two-factor authentication (2FA).

4. Secure Your Private Keys: Generate and securely store your private keys or seed

phrase. Private keys are crucial for accessing and managing your digital assets. Hardware wallets often provide an extra layer of security by keeping private keys offline.

5. Fund Your Wallet: Once your wallet is set up, you can add funds by purchasing cryptocurrencies from reputable exchanges or receiving them from other wallet addresses. Ensure you follow best practices for safe and secure transactions.

6. Regularly Update and Backup: Keep your wallet software up to date with the latest security patches and features. Regularly back up your wallet and private keys to ensure the safety of your funds in case of device loss or failure.

Regarding security, consider some of the best practices. Use Strong Authentication. Enable 2FA (Two-Factor Authentication) whenever possible, adding an extra layer of protection to your wallet. This typically involves using an authentication app or receiving codes via SMS or email.

Secondly, stay Vigilant Against Scams. Be cautious of phishing attempts, malicious websites, and fraudulent schemes targeting cryptocurrency users. Always verify the authenticity of websites, links, and software before providing sensitive information.

Thirdly, keep your software up to date. Update your wallet software regularly to benefit from the latest security enhancements and bug fixes.

And, lastly, store your info offline. For added

security, consider keeping a copy of your private keys or seed phrase in offline storage, such as a hardware wallet or a secure physical location. Regularly back up your wallet to protect against data loss.

To boil it down to one final statement: Setting up a digital wallet for cryptocurrency is an essential step for individuals seeking to engage in the world of digital finance. By understanding the various types of wallets available, following the step-by-step setup process, and implementing security best practices, users can enjoy the benefits of secure and convenient cryptocurrency transactions. Embracing this technology empowers individuals to take control of their financial future in the evolving digital landscape.

Exploring Different Types of Cryptocurrencies and their Features

Cryptocurrencies have revolutionized the world of finance, introducing a decentralized and secure digital medium of exchange. Since the advent of Bitcoin, numerous cryptocurrencies have emerged, each with unique features and purposes. The following information aims to explore the various types of cryptocurrencies and shed light on their distinctive characteristics, use-cases, and technological innovations.

I. Bitcoin and Digital Gold: Bitcoin, the pioneer of cryptocurrencies, introduced the concept of a decentralized digital currency built on blockchain technology. It serves as a store of value and a medium of exchange. Bitcoin's key features include scarcity, as it has a limited supply of 21 million coins, and security through cryptographic algorithms. Its decentralized nature ensures transparency and resistance to censorship.

II. Smart Contract Platforms:
1. Ethereum (ETH): Ethereum is a decentralized platform that enables the development of smart contracts and decentralized applications (DApps). It introduced the concept of programmable money, allowing developers to build and deploy applications on its blockchain. Ethereum's native cryptocurrency, Ether, serves as a fuel for executing smart contracts and powering the platform.
2. Binance Smart Chain (BSC): Binance is a smart contract platform. Known as a Smart Chain, it serves as a parallel blockchain to the Binance Chain, designed to facilitate the creation of decentralized applications and tokens. BSC offers high performance and low transaction fees, making it an attractive option for developers. Its native cryptocurrency, Binance Coin (BNB), is used for transactions and governance within the Binance ecosystem.

III. Privacy-Centric Cryptocurrencies:

1. Monero (XMR): Monero focuses on privacy and anonymity, utilizing advanced cryptographic techniques to obfuscate transaction details. It employs ring signatures, stealth addresses, and confidential transactions to enhance privacy. Monero's privacy features make it difficult to trace transactions and identify the individuals involved.

2. Zcash (ZEC): Zcash is another privacy-oriented cryptocurrency that employs zero-knowledge proofs called zk-SNARKs. These proofs allow users to verify transactions without revealing the sender, recipient, or transaction amount. Zcash provides users with the option to shield transactions for enhanced privacy or keep them transparent.

IV. Stablecoins: Stablecoins are cryptocurrencies designed to minimize price volatility by pegging their value to external assets such as fiat currencies or commodities. They offer stability and can be used as a medium of exchange and a store of value. Some popular stablecoins include Tether (USDT), USD Coin (USDC), and Dai (DAI).

V. Utility Tokens: Utility tokens are cryptocurrencies that provide access to a specific product or service within a blockchain ecosystem. They serve as a medium of exchange on decentralized platforms, granting holders various privileges, such as voting rights or access to discounted services. Examples include Basic Attention Token (BAT) used in the Brave browser and Chainlink (LINK) used for decentralized oracle services.

VI. Asset-Backed Cryptocurrencies: Asset-backed cryptocurrencies derive their value from underlying physical or digital assets. They aim to bridge the gap between traditional finance and the digital world. For instance, Tether (USDT) is pegged to the value of the U.S. dollar, offering stability and facilitating easy conversion between cryptocurrencies and fiat currencies.

To summarize: The world of cryptocurrencies encompasses a diverse range of digital assets, each with its unique features, purposes, and technological advancements. Bitcoin paved the way for decentralized digital currencies, while platforms like Ethereum introduced programmability and smart contracts. Privacy-centric cryptocurrencies prioritize anonymity, stablecoins provide stability, utility tokens grant access to platforms, and asset-backed cryptocurrencies bridge the gap between traditional and digital finance. Understanding the characteristics and applications of different cryptocurrencies empowers individuals to navigate and leverage this evolving landscape, unlocking new possibilities for financial transactions and technological innovations.

CRYPTOCURRENCY FOR SENIORS

Choosing a Reputable Cryptocurrency Exchange Platform

With the growing popularity and adoption of cryptocurrencies, choosing a reputable cryptocurrency exchange platform is crucial for individuals looking to buy, sell, and trade digital assets. The right platform can provide a secure and reliable environment for transactions, ensuring the safety of funds and offering a seamless user experience. This section aims to outline key factors to consider when selecting a reputable cryptocurrency exchange platform.

Look for platforms that operate within legal frameworks and adhere to regulatory requirements. Compliance with know-your-customer (KYC) and anti-money laundering (AML) regulations indicates a commitment to maintaining a transparent and secure environment.

Strong security measures, such as 2FA (which stands for Two-Factor Authentication), add an extra layer of protection to user accounts. Platforms that offer multiple authentication methods, such as SMS verification, authenticator apps, or hardware keys, prioritize user security.

In addition, consider exchanges that utilize cold storage for the majority of their funds. Cold storage keeps cryptocurrencies offline, reducing the risk of hacking and unauthorized access.

Research user reviews and feedback on reputable platforms, considering factors such as reliability, customer support, and ease of use. Reliable sources like online forums, social media platforms, and trusted review websites can provide valuable insights into a platform's reputation.

Furthermore, evaluate the platform's operational history and track record. Established exchanges with a proven track record are more likely to provide a secure and trustworthy trading environment.

Moreover, look for exchanges that maintain transparency in their operations, including openly sharing information about their team, legal compliance, security practices, and partnerships. Transparent platforms build trust and demonstrate their commitment to accountability.

Likewise, consider exchanges that offer high liquidity, as this ensures that you can easily buy or sell cryptocurrencies at fair prices without significant slippage. Higher liquidity also contributes to a smoother trading experience.

Assess the range of available trading pairs on the platform. (The term "trading pair" refers to when you have two cryptocurrencies that can be traded against each other in a market. The first cryptocurrency listed in the pair is referred to as the base currency or base asset, while the second cryptocurrency is called the quote currency or quote asset. For example, on a popular exchange like Binance, you might see trading pairs such as BTC/ETH, ETH/USDT, or XRP/BTC. In the BTC/ETH pair, Bitcoin (BTC) is the base currency, and Ethereum (ETH) is the quote currency. This means that when trading in this pair, the exchange rate is based on the value of ETH relative to

BTC.)

The more diverse the selection of trading pairs, the greater the opportunities for trading and diversification. Ensure that the platform supports the cryptocurrencies you intend to trade.

Also be sure to look for platforms with a user-friendly interface that offers a seamless trading experience. A well-designed and intuitive interface simplifies the process of placing orders, monitoring market movements, and managing funds.

Consider the platform's responsiveness and trading speed. A reliable exchange should be capable of handling high trading volumes without significant lags or downtime.

If you prefer trading on-the-go, consider platforms that provide mobile applications or responsive mobile web interfaces. Mobile accessibility offers convenience and flexibility.

Also evaluate the quality and availability of customer support provided by the exchange. Look for platforms that offer multiple channels of communication, such as live chat, email, or phone support. Prompt and knowledgeable customer support can assist in resolving any issues or concerns that may arise during your trading journey.

As your knowledge-base grows, you may also start to look into other factors that align with your specific needs, such as margin trading options, educational resources, community engagement, or access to advanced trading features. These additional features can enhance your trading experience and help you achieve your investment goals.

There are several reputable cryptocurrency exchanges available in the market. While it's important to conduct thorough research and consider individual needs and preferences, here is a list of well-established and reputable exchanges:

1. Binance
2. Coinbase Pro
3. Kraken
4. Bitstamp
5. Gemini
6. Bittrex
7. KuCoin
8. Huobi Global
9. OKEx
10. Bitfinex

These exchanges have gained recognition for their security measures, regulatory compliance, user experience, liquidity, and overall reliability. However, it's important to note that the cryptocurrency market is dynamic, and reputation can change over time, so it is advisable to conduct up-to-date research and read user reviews before choosing an exchange.

Conclusion

Choosing a reputable cryptocurrency exchange platform is paramount to ensuring the security, reliability, and overall trading experience within the digital asset ecosystem. By considering factors such as security measures, reputation, liquidity, user experience, and customer support, individuals can make informed decisions when selecting an exchange. Remember to conduct thorough research, assess your own requirements, and prioritize platforms that align with your trading goals. A reputable exchange can serve as a reliable gateway to the world of cryptocurrencies, enabling you to participate in this transformative financial landscape with confidence.

Chapter Three

*Explaining the Concept of Bitcoin and
its Historical Significance*

Bitcoin, the first and most prominent cryptocurrency, has revolutionized the world of finance and digital transactions since its introduction in 2009. Bitcoin introduced the concept of decentralized digital currency built on blockchain technology. It has had a transformative impact on the global financial landscape. One of its key revolutionary features is its decentralization. Eliminating the need for intermediaries like banks or governments, it utilizes the aforementioned blockchain technology: a distributed ledger that records all transactions in a transparent and immutable manner. This technology ensures transparency, security, and resistance to censorship.

Bitcoin relies on cryptographic algorithms to secure transactions and control the creation of new units. Public-key cryptography enables the creation of unique digital signatures that verify the authenticity of transactions and the ownership of Bitcoin units.

One of the cryptocurrency's most attractive features is the fact that it has a finite supply capped at 21 million coins, making it resistant to inflation.

Consider the Federal Reserve's target-rate of 2% inflation.(For a rule of thumb, remember that banker's love inflation. Deflation, by contrast, is not so good for central banks.) The objective for the Fed is a 2% inflation rate.

But understand that, for the consumer, this could have corrosive effects over a long time-horizon. For instance, over a 30-year period with a 2% inflation rate, the value of $1,000 would be eroded to approximately $1,811.60. This means that the purchasing power of the initial amount would decrease by about 45.8% due to inflation.

And that's just with a 2% inflation rate!

Imagine a 4% rate! Or a 9% rate!

As the global economy experiences unprecedented turbulence due to the natural entropy of fiat currencies, Bitcoin has become quite attractive to many investors.

Resistant to inflation, new Bitcoins are created through a process called mining, where powerful computers compete to solve complex mathematical problems. Mining not only generates new coins but also validates transactions and maintains the security of the network.

Beginning on January 3, 2009, with the mining of its genesis block, Bitcoin emerged in the aftermath of the 2008 global financial crisis. This was a time of eroding trust in traditional financial systems. Bitcoin's decentralized nature and resistance to censorship appealed to those seeking an alternative to centralized banking systems.

Its launch paved the way for the development of thousands of other cryptocurrencies, collectively known as altcoins. It provided a blueprint for subsequent projects and demonstrated the viability of decentralized digital currencies.

Over time, Bitcoin gained mainstream recognition and acceptance. Major companies and institutions started acknowledging its potential, with some even incorporating it into their operations. Notable examples include Tesla's investment in Bitcoin and the acceptance of Bitcoin as a payment method by various merchants and organizations. Other companies that accept it (as of the writing of this book) are Microsoft, Cheapair, Newegg, Starbucks, Subway, Gyft, Home Depot, Twitch, AT&T, Burger King, KFC, Expedia, Webjet, and the list goes on and on.

Bitcoin has the potential to provide financial services to the unbanked and underbanked populations worldwide, bypassing traditional financial barriers. Its accessibility allows individuals to store, send, and receive funds securely, regardless of geographical location or existing financial infrastructure.

Its borderless nature and lower transaction fees compared to traditional methods make it an attractive option for cross-border remittances. It enables faster and cheaper international transactions, potentially reducing reliance on costly intermediaries.

Because of all these features, Bitcoin poses challenges to traditional the banking system by offering an alternative form of value storage and transfer. As individuals gain more control over their financial assets, the need for traditional banking services may decrease, leading to potential disruptions in the banking industry.

Bitcoin's underlying blockchain technology has inspired further innovations and developments in various industries beyond finance. It has sparked the exploration of blockchain applications in supply chain management, voting systems, identity verification, and more.

Nothing is perfect, though. Bitcoin's price volatility remains a significant challenge, hindering its adoption as a stable medium of exchange. Additionally, regulatory frameworks around cryptocurrencies are still evolving, leading to uncertainty and potential limitations on its usage.

In addition, Bitcoin faces scalability issues, with limitations on the number of transactions the network can handle. Addressing scalability while minimizing the environmental impact of Bitcoin mining's energy consumption remains a focus for ongoing development and innovation.

As the cryptocurrency market continues to evolve, Bitcoin's role may shift. It may coexist with other cryptocurrencies, and its significance may extend beyond a store of value to encompass broader financial services and applications.

The bottom line: Bitcoin, as the pioneering crypto-currency, has revolutionized the financial world by introducing a decentralized digital currency system. Its historical significance lies in challenging traditional financial systems, fostering financial inclusion, and sparking technological innovations. While Bitcoin has faced challenges such as volatility and regulatory concerns, its impact on the global financial landscape remains significant. As cryptocurrencies and blockchain technology continue to develop, Bitcoin's journey will continue to shape the future of finance, empowering individuals with increased control over their financial assets and offering alternative avenues for economic participation.

Discussing the Process of Bitcoin Mining and Transactions

Bitcoin mining and transactions form the backbone of the Bitcoin network, enabling the creation of new coins and facilitating secure and transparent peer-to-peer transactions. For any new investor to understand these processes in greater depth, it might be prudent to start with some fundamentals. To shed light on the significance and the underlying technologies involved, we'll begin with Bitcoin mining: the concept and the purpose.

Bitcoin mining refers to the process of validating transactions, securing the network, and adding new blocks to the blockchain. Miners, using powerful computers, compete to solve complex mathematical puzzles, known as proof-of-work (PoW), in order to mine new Bitcoins.

The PoW algorithm requires miners to make numerous attempts by solving computationally intensive mathematical problems. The goal is to find a specific value, known as a nonce, that, when combined with other block data, produces a hash with a predefined number of leading zeros. This process is resource-intensive and time-consuming, ensuring that miners invest computational power to secure the network.

Once a miner successfully solves the PoW puzzle, they create a new block containing a set of verified transactions. This block is added to the existing blockchain, creating an immutable record of all transactions. Miners are rewarded with newly minted Bitcoins and transaction fees for their efforts.

Transactions occur when users send or receive Bitcoins. To initiate a transaction, a user creates a digital signature using their private key to prove ownership of the funds. The transaction is then broadcast to the network for verification.

Verified transactions enter the mempool, a temporary holding area where pending transactions await confirmation by miners. The mempool serves as a pool of unconfirmed transactions available for selection in the creation of new blocks.

Miners select transactions from the mempool and include them in a new block they are attempting to mine. Once a block is mined, it is added to the blockchain, and the transactions within it are considered confirmed. As more blocks are added to the blockchain, the number of confirmations for a transaction increases, strengthening its immutability.

Users can choose to attach transaction fees to incentivize miners to prioritize their transactions. Transaction fees are typically voluntary and serve as an incentive for miners to include the transaction in a block. Higher fees increase the likelihood of faster confirmation.

The Bitcoin network relies on a decentralized peer-to-peer system where multiple participants validate and agree on the state of the blockchain. Through consensus mechanisms, such as the longest-chain rule, all nodes in the network reach a consensus on the valid chain, ensuring the integrity and immutability of transactions.

The blockchain provides a transparent and secure ledger of all Bitcoin transactions. Each block in the chain contains a reference to the previous block, creating a cryptographic link that makes it extremely difficult to alter or tamper with the recorded transactions.

Bitcoin's blockchain is an example of a distributed ledger, where copies of the blockchain are stored on multiple computers (nodes) across the network. This distributed nature enhances security, as altering a single copy of the blockchain would require altering the majority of copies held by independent nodes.

There are, of course, challenges and future considerations regarding this emergent technology. For one (as alluded to before), Bitcoin mining is energy-intensive, leading to concerns about its environmental impact. Efforts are being made to develop more energy-efficient mining methods and explore alternative consensus mechanisms, such as proof-of-stake (PoS), which consumes less energy.

(Incidentally, Bitcoin does not currently utilize the proof-of-stake system. Proof-of-Stake is an alternative consensus mechanism employed by some cryptocurrencies, including Ethereum 2.0 and Cardano. In a PoS system, validators are chosen to create new blocks and validate transactions based on the number of coins they hold and are willing to "stake" as collateral. The selection of validators is typically based on a random or deterministic process that considers their stake's size and age.)

As Bitcoin's popularity and transaction-volume increase, scalability becomes a challenge. Innovations, like the Lightning Network, aim to address scalability issues by enabling faster and more scalable off-chain transactions.

Bitcoin's mining and transaction processes continue to evolve as new technologies and improvements are introduced. Segregated Witness (SegWit), for instance, increased transaction capacity and introduced new scripting capabilities.

The long and the short of it is: Bitcoin mining and transactions form the foundation of the Bitcoin network, facilitating secure, transparent, and decentralized peer-to-peer transactions. The mining process involves solving complex mathematical puzzles to validate transactions and add them to the blockchain. Transactions undergo verification, inclusion in the mempool, and confirmation through block inclusion. Blockchain technology ensures decentralization, security, and transparency, providing a trustworthy record of all Bitcoin transactions. As Bitcoin continues to evolve, addressing challenges such as energy consumption and scalability, its mining and transaction processes will likely adapt, paving the way for a more efficient and accessible digital currency ecosystem.

Examining the Potential Uses and Future of Bitcoin

Although Bitcoin's *primary* use-case is as a digital currency for online transactions, its potential in e-commerce and online peer-to-peer transactions remains significant.

In addition, Bitcoin has the potential to simplify and expedite cross-border transactions, eliminating the need for multiple intermediaries and reducing transfer fees and transaction settlement times. It offers a viable solution for remittances, providing financial inclusion and cost-effective alternatives for individuals in regions with limited access to traditional banking services.

It's also a hedge against inflation—especially for those sending money across borders. Bitcoin's limited supply and deflationary nature make it an attractive store of value, particularly in regions experiencing high inflation or economic instability. Purchasing power is preserved from the erosion caused by fiat currency devaluation.

So as people choose to retire to different countries (an increasingly popular phenomenon for seniors choosing to spend their sunset years on the sandy beaches of some tropical locale), they can have greater confidence that their nest egg won't suffer the erosion it otherwise would in the older fiat-based financial system.

Of particular concern to seniors is the protection of the value of their portfolios. As an emerging asset class, Bitcoin offers a potential hedge against market volatility and an avenue for portfolio diversification, providing exposure to a different risk-reward profile.

Moreover, Bitcoin's programmable money capabilities, through technologies like smart contracts or second-layer solutions, can enable the development of decentralized financial applications. Bitcoin-based DeFi (Decentralized Finance) solutions could provide services such as lending, borrowing, decentralized exchanges, and yield farming.

In passing, it might be good to point out that "yield farming," also known as liquidity mining, is a concept that emerged within the decentralized finance (DeFi) ecosystem and involves earning rewards by providing liquidity to specific cryptocurrency protocols. While yield farming encompasses a range of strategies, the fundamental principle revolves around utilizing deposited funds to generate additional returns. Yield farming has gained popularity due to its potential for high returns compared to traditional financial instruments. However, it is a highly specialized and often complex strategy that requires careful understanding and risk management.

At any rate . . .

Bitcoin's success has propelled wider recognition and adoption of blockchain technology across various industries. Cryptocurrencies notwithstanding, Blockchain applications (as mentioned previously) are now being adopted in sectors such as supply chain management, identity verification, and voting systems. Bitcoin's future lies not only in its own development but also in its influence on blockchain innovation.

Conclusion

Bitcoin's potential uses and future prospects extend far beyond its role as a digital currency. It holds promise as a medium of exchange, store of value, and transformative technology in various sectors. With its growing adoption, Bitcoin could reshape financial systems, foster financial inclusion, and drive technological advancements. However, challenges related to scalability, regulatory frameworks, and environmental sustainability must be addressed. As Bitcoin continues to mature, it will likely navigate these challenges, leading to a future where cryptocurrencies play an increasingly integral role in the global economy.

Chapter Four

*Introducing Alternative Cryptocurrencies
and their Unique Features*

With that overview of Bitcoin out of the way, now it's time to explore other altcoins and tokens. These alternative cryptocurrencies aim to offer unique improvements or innovations compared to Bitcoin. We'll now explore a selection of alternative coins and delve into their distinctive features, use-cases, and potential impact on the broader crypto ecosystem.

First stop: Ethereum. It introduced the concept of programmable money through its robust smart contract functionality. It allows developers to create and deploy decentralized applications that can execute complex logic and automate agreements, expanding the potential use-cases of blockchain technology beyond digital currency.

The EVM (Ethereum Virtual Machine) enables developers to write and deploy smart contracts in various programming languages. It serves as the runtime environment for executing smart contracts on the Ethereum network, fostering a vibrant ecosystem of DApps and decentralized finance (DeFi) applications.

Next, let's talk about Ripple. Ripple aims to revolutionize the traditional cross-border payment system by providing fast and low-cost international transactions. Its payment protocol, RippleNet, facilitates efficient transfer of various assets, including fiat currencies, cryptocurrencies, and commodities.

Ripple utilizes a unique consensus mechanism called the Ripple Protocol Consensus Algorithm (RPCA). Unlike Bitcoin's energy-intensive proof-of-work (PoW), RPCA relies on a network of trusted validators to verify transactions, resulting in faster confirmation-times and reduced energy consumption.

Next in our overview comes Cardano, Cardano emphasizes academic research and peer-reviewed development. The project places great importance on scientific rigor, formal methods, and evidence-based approaches to enhance security, scalability, and sustainability.

Cardano employs a PoS consensus mechanism called Ouroboros. It aims to be more energy-efficient than PoW systems while maintaining security and decentralization. Cardano's PoS approach involves a strong emphasis on governance and stakeholder participation in decision-making processes.

Another cryptocurrency that's making waves is Litecoin. It's often referred to as the "silver" to Bitcoin's "gold," and offers faster block generation times and transaction confirmations. It employs a different hashing algorithm called Scrypt, enabling quicker validation and improving overall transaction speed.

Litecoin was among the first cryptocurrencies to adopt SegWit, a protocol upgrade that enhances scalability and transaction efficiency. SegWit separates transaction signatures from transaction data, allowing more transactions to fit within a single block.

Another emergency currency is Monero. Monero focuses on privacy and anonymity by implementing advanced cryptographic techniques such as ring signatures and stealth addresses. These features obfuscate transaction details, making it significantly more challenging to trace or link transactions to specific individuals.

Monero uses the aforementioned ring signatures to mix a user's transaction with multiple decoy transactions, making it difficult to determine the actual sender. Additionally, the implementation of confidential transactions conceals the transaction amounts, further enhancing privacy and fungibility.

Another cryptocurrency in the financial ecosystem is Polkadot. Polkadot aims to address the issue of blockchain interoperability by facilitating communication and data transfer between different blockchains. It provides a framework for creating and connecting multiple specialized blockchains, enabling cross-chain transfers and enhancing scalability and functionality.

Polkadot's security model, known as "shared security," allows smaller or newer blockchains to leverage the security provided by the larger Polkadot network. This approach reduces the barriers to entry for new blockchain projects while maintaining a robust security framework.

There are, of course, many, *many* new altcoins out

there (and more are coming on the scene everyday). This is just a select menu, but you can go online and do further research. This thumbnail sketch was just to whet your appetite and make you aware of some of the key players, unique features and innovations emerging on the scene. Ethereum revolutionized smart contracts and decentralized applications, Ripple streamlined cross-border payments, and Cardano prioritized scientific research and PoS consensus. Litecoin enhanced transaction speed, Monero prioritized privacy and fungibility, while Polkadot aimed to foster blockchain interoperability. Each alternative cryptocurrency contributes to the broader crypto ecosystem, expanding possibilities and driving innovation in various sectors. As the market continues to evolve, these altcoins showcase the diversity and potential for growth in the cryptocurrency landscape, shaping the future of digital currencies and blockchain technology.

Understanding the Differences Between Tokens and Coins

In the realm of cryptocurrencies, the terms "tokens" and "coins" are frequently used, often interchangeably. However, they represent distinct concepts within the cryptocurrency ecosystem. Let's look into some of the differences between them, exploring their definitions, characteristics, and use-cases.

To begin with, tokens are digital assets built on existing blockchain platforms, such as Ethereum or

Binance Smart Chain. They represent programmable units of value and function within specific ecosystems or applications. Tokenization involves the creation of digital representations of real-world or digital assets. These tokens are often designed to have utility or represent ownership rights in a specific project, platform, or decentralized application (DApp).

Tokens are typically created and managed using smart contracts, self-executing agreements coded on blockchain networks. Smart contracts define the token's functionality, supply, distribution, and other parameters.

Contrasted with tokens are coins. Coins, also known as cryptocurrencies, represent native currencies that operate on their independent blockchain networks. Unlike tokens, coins are stand-alone entities with their own blockchain and do not rely on existing platforms.

Coins have their own underlying infrastructure, consensus mechanisms, and governance systems. Some of the examples we already covered include Bitcoin (BTC), Ethereum (ETH), and Litecoin (LTC), which have dedicated blockchains and serve as mediums of exchange and stores of value.

Coins primarily serve as digital currencies, designed for peer-to-peer transactions, value storage, and unit of account. They are often used as a medium of exchange, enabling users to purchase goods and services directly or trade on cryptocurrency exchanges.

One of the other differentiating characteristics between coins and tokens is functionality. Tokens are programmable and versatile, capable of representing various assets, rights, or functionalities within specific platforms or applications. Coins, on the other hand, primarily serve as currencies and are used for general transactions.

Tokens rely on existing blockchain platforms, utilizing their infrastructure and consensus mechanisms. In contrast, coins operate on their own blockchain networks, which are typically designed specifically for their use-case.

Coins are often introduced through mining or pre-mined distributions, where a portion of the initial coin supply is allocated to founders or early adopters. Tokens, however, are usually created through initial coin offerings (ICOs), token sales, or airdrops, offering access or ownership rights within a particular ecosystem.

Tokens have diverse applications, including utility tokens that enable access to specific services, security tokens representing ownership or investment in real-world assets, and governance tokens that allow participation in decision-making processes within decentralized platforms.

Regarding use-cases, coins primarily serve as digital currencies, facilitating transactions, store of value, and enabling participation in decentralized networks. Bitcoin (BTC) acts as a decentralized digital currency, Ethereum (ETH) powers smart contracts and DApps, and Litecoin (LTC) offers fast and low-cost transactions.

With respect to regulatory considerations, some tokens, particularly security tokens, may fall under regulatory frameworks governing securities. These tokens may require compliance with securities laws, such as registration or qualification, to ensure investor protection.

Coins, as stand-alone cryptocurrencies, often face regulatory scrutiny and may be subject to regulations relating to anti-money laundering (AML), know-your-customer (KYC), and financial services.

In summary: Tokens and coins represent two distinct categories within the cryptocurrency ecosystem. (To take an analogy from the older financial system, think of the difference between cash and securities.) But to be more specific: Tokens are versatile and programmable, representing various assets, rights, or functionalities, whereas coins primarily function as digital currencies. Understanding the differences between tokens and coins is crucial for navigating the evolving landscape of cryptocurrencies, their use-cases, and the regulatory considerations that apply to each category. As the cryptocurrency space continues to mature, both tokens and coins will play pivotal roles in shaping the future of digital finance and decentralized applications.

Discussing Popular Altcoins and their Potential Applications

The cryptocurrency market has expanded beyond Bitcoin, with numerous alternative cryptocurrencies, commonly known as altcoins, gaining traction. These altcoins offer unique features, innovations, and potential applications in various sectors. Now, we'll take a moment to explore some popular altcoins and their potential applications, highlighting their distinct characteristics and the impact they may have on the broader crypto landscape.

Ethereum, we mentioned before. To reiterate, it introduced the concept of programmable money, enabling the creation and execution of smart contracts. This functionality allows developers to build decentralized applications (DApps) with various use- cases, including decentralized finance (DeFi), supply chain management, and identity verification.

Ethereum's platform facilitates the creation of tokens, enabling projects to conduct initial coin offerings (ICOs) for fundraising. This has spurred the growth of tokenized assets, utility tokens, and security tokens, opening avenues for token-based crowdfunding, ownership rights representation, and ecosystem participation.

We also hit upon Ripple earlier. Just to refresh your memory, Ripple focuses on cross-border remittances and payment systems by providing fast, low-cost, and efficient transactions. Its technology, RippleNet, enables financial institutions to settle cross-border transactions quickly, leveraging XRP as a bridge currency for liquidity and reducing costs associated with traditional intermediaries.

Ripple has forged partnerships with various banks and financial institutions, offering them access to its blockchain-based solutions. These partnerships enhance the speed and efficiency of global transactions and improve liquidity management for financial institutions.

The altcoin known as Cardano emphasizes scientific research and formal methods, aiming to provide a secure, scalable, and sustainable blockchain platform. Through its rigorous development approach, Cardano aims to address challenges related to scalability, interoperability, and governance in blockchain technology.

Cardano seeks to enable decentralized finance (DeFi) applications while addressing scalability and sustainability concerns. Additionally, Cardano aims to foster social impact initiatives, utilizing blockchain technology to improve transparency, accountability, and efficiency in areas such as supply chain management and identity verification.

The new cryptocurrency Polkadot addresses the challenge of interoperability by facilitating communication and data-sharing between different blockchains. It enables the transfer of assets and data across different networks, enhancing scalability, functionality, and collaboration among blockchain projects.

Polkadot's architecture introduces the concept of

parachains, which are individual blockchains connected to the Polkadot relay chain. Parachains can be developed using the Substrate framework, enabling developers to build customized blockchains with specific features, use- cases, and governance mechanisms.

Chainlink, by contrast, specializes in providing decentralized oracle networks, which facilitate the connection between on-chain smart contracts and off-chain data sources. Oracles play a vital role in accessing real-world data, enabling smart contracts to interact with external systems, such as price feeds, weather data, and other APIs.

Chainlink's oracle technology is particularly valuable in the decentralized finance (DeFi) space, where accurate and reliable external data is essential for various financial applications. Additionally, Chainlink's oracles have potential applications in supply chain management, insurance, and gaming.

Binance Coin serves as the native cryptocurrency of the Binance exchange. It offers utility and benefits within the Binance ecosystem, including discounted trading fees, participation in token sales on the Binance Launchpad, and access to various Binance services.

Binance periodically burns a portion of BNB tokens, reducing the circulating supply and potentially increasing the value of remaining tokens. This deflationary mechanism aims to create scarcity and drive demand for BNB.

Conclusion

Popular altcoins, such as Ethereum, Ripple, Cardano, Polkadot, Chainlink, and Binance Coin, have garnered attention and demonstrated potential applications beyond traditional cryptocurrencies. Ethereum enables the creation of smart contracts and decentralized applications, while Ripple focuses on revolutionizing cross-border payments. Cardano emphasizes scientific research and social impact initiatives. Polkadot enhances interoperability and collaboration among blockchains. Chainlink provides secure and reliable oracle solutions, and Binance Coin serves as the utility token within the Binance ecosystem. These altcoins showcase the diverse use-cases and innovations within the cryptocurrency space, paving the way for transformative applications in decentralized finance (DeFi), supply chain management, identity verification, and more. As the altcoin market evolves, these projects contribute to the ongoing development of blockchain technology and the expansion of its real-world applications.

Chapter Five
Buying and Selling Cryptocurrency

As the popularity of cryptocurrencies continues to rise, more individuals are becoming interested in purchasing these digital assets. This step-by-step guide aims to provide a comprehensive overview of the process involved in purchasing cryptocurrencies. From setting up a digital wallet to selecting a reputable cryptocurrency exchange and executing a purchase, this guide will help newcomers navigate the world of cryptocurrency investments.

Step 1: Educate yourself. Start by researching and familiarizing yourself with the basics of cryptocurrencies. (The fact that you're reading this book is an indication that you're already well on your way.) But don't stop here. Continue learning about different types of cryptocurrencies, their underlying technologies, and the potential risks and benefits associated with investing in them.

After you've done your due diligence, decide which specific cryptocurrency you want to purchase. Consider factors such as its purpose, market capitalization, historical performance, and potential for future growth. It's advisable to diversify your portfolio by considering a mix of well-established cryptocurrencies and promising newcomers.

Step 2: Set Up a Digital Wallet. Select one that suits your needs. There are various types of wallets, including (as we discussed before) hardware wallets, software wallets, and web wallets. Hardware wallets, such as Ledger or Trezor, offer enhanced security, while software and web wallets provide convenience but may be more susceptible to hacking risks.

Even though it's not a comprehensive list, here are a few options:

1. Hardware Wallets:
    o Ledger Nano S
    o Ledger Nano X
    o Trezor Model T
    o Trezor One
    o KeepKey
2. Software Wallets:
    o Exodus
    o Atomic Wallet
    o Electrum
    o MyEtherWallet (MEW)
    o Trust Wallet
3. Mobile Wallets:
    o Coinbase Wallet
    o MetaMask (available as a browser extension and mobile app)
    o Edge Wallet
    o Coinomi
    o BRD (Bread Wallet)
4. Web Wallets:
    o MyEtherWallet (MEW)

- o MetaMask (available as a browser extension and mobile app)
- o Trust Wallet (also available as a browser extension)
- o Coinomi
- o Guarda Wallet

5. Paper Wallets (Cold Storage):
   - o Bitaddress.org
   - o WalletGenerator.net
   - o MyEtherWallet (MEW) (can generate paper wallets)

6. Multi-Currency Wallets:
   - a. Exodus
   - b. Coinomi
   - c. Trust Wallet
   - d. Atomic Wallet
   - e. Jaxx Liberty

Once you decide which type of wallet suits your needs, follow the instructions given by the wallet provider to set it up. This usually involves creating a strong password, securing your wallet's private keys, and enabling two-factor authentication (2FA) for added security.

Step 3: Choose a Cryptocurrency Exchange. Conduct thorough research to identify reputable exchanges that support the cryptocurrency you wish to purchase. Look for exchanges with a solid reputation, user-friendly interfaces, robust security measures, and good customer support.

Once you do that, create an account on the chosen exchange by providing the required personal information. This typically includes verifying your identity through a Know Your Customer (KYC) process, which may involve submitting identification documents and proof of address.

Step 4: Fund Your Exchange Account. Once your account is set up and verified, deposit funds into your exchange account. This is usually done by linking a bank account or using other available payment methods, such as credit or debit cards, bank transfers, or even other cryptocurrencies.

Next, enable security measures. Learn what features are offered by the exchange, such as two-factor authentication (2FA) and withdrawal whitelist settings. These measures help protect your funds and provide an extra layer of security.

Step 5: Place an Order. Select the trading pair that matches the cryptocurrency you want to purchase with your desired currency. For example, if you want to buy Bitcoin (BTC), you may need to choose the BTC/USD or BTC/EUR trading pair.

Next, decide whether you want to place a market order or a limit order. A market order executes the trade immediately at the current market price, while a limit order allows you to specify the price at which you want to buy the cryptocurrency.

Step 6: Safely store your cryptocurrencies. Once your purchase is complete, it is advisable to transfer your cryptocurrencies from the exchange to your personal digital wallet. This ensures that you have full control and ownership of your assets, reducing the risk of them being compromised on the exchange.

In addition, it may be smart to take appropriate measures to back up your wallet and store the backup in a secure location. This is essential in case of any loss or damage to your device or if you forget your wallet password.

To make a long story short: Purchasing cryptocurrencies can be an exciting and potentially rewarding venture. By following this step-by-step guide, you can navigate the process with confidence. Remember to conduct thorough research, set up a secure digital wallet, choose a reputable cryptocurrency exchange, fund your account, place an order, and ensure the safe storage of your purchased cryptocurrencies. As with any investment, it is crucial to exercise caution, diversify your portfolio, and stay informed about the ever-evolving cryptocurrency market.

Exploring Different Payment Methods and Security Considerations

The process of buying and selling cryptocurrency involves a range of payment methods and requires careful attention to security considerations. As the cryptocurrency market continues to grow, individuals are seeking convenient and secure ways to engage in transactions. Toward that end, let's explore different payment methods for buying and selling cryptocurrency and discuss essential security considerations to ensure a safe and reliable experience.

First, let's start with considering payment methods for buying cryptocurrency. To begin with, you'll probably seize upon what you're used to—namely, fiat currency. You're in luck, because many cryptocurrency exchanges accept traditional fiat currencies, such as USD, EUR, or GBP. Payment methods for fiat deposits often include bank transfers, credit or debit card payments, and payment processors like PayPal or Skrill. These methods provide easy access for individuals transitioning from traditional finance to the world of cryptocurrencies.

Another way to acquire cryptocurrencies, however, is through cryptocurrency-to-cryptocurrency exchanges. These exchanges facilitate trading between different cryptocurrencies, allowing users to convert one cryptocurrency into another. This method often requires users to already own a cryptocurrency and use it to acquire another.

Peer-to-peer platforms offer another option. They enable direct transactions between individuals without the involvement of a centralized exchange. Users can buy cryptocurrencies directly from sellers using various payment methods, including bank transfers, digital wallets, and even cash in some cases. P2P platforms offer more flexibility and can cater to specific payment preferences.

Now that we've gotten buying out of the way, let's consider selling.

Some payment methods for selling include (of course) fiat currency. When selling cryptocurrency, individuals often want to convert their digital assets back into fiat currency. Cryptocurrency exchanges typically provide options to withdraw funds directly to bank accounts via wire transfers or other payment processors. These withdrawals involve converting cryptocurrencies into fiat currency and sending the funds to the designated bank account.

Peer-to-Peer (P2P) platforms also facilitate the selling of cryptocurrencies, allowing individuals to connect directly with buyers. Sellers can receive payment in fiat currency or other agreed-upon payment methods. P2P platforms provide an alternative to traditional exchanges, offering more control over the selling process.

To recap: Some of the payment options when selling cryptos are bank transfers, PayPal, digital payment platforms, other cryptocurrencies, prepaid cards or vouchers . . . and, of course, your local national fiat currency.

Now on to security considerations . . .

First thing's first: choosing a secure exchange. Prioritize security when selecting a cryptocurrency exchange. Look for platforms with robust security measures, such as two-factor authentication (2FA), cold storage for funds, encryption protocols, and a strong track record of protecting user assets. Research the exchange's reputation, reviews, and security incidents to make an informed decision. (Some places you can go for reviews are Trustpilot, Bitcointalk, Cryptocompare, CoinMarketCap, et al.)

Step two: safeguard your cryptocurrency by using

secure wallets. As we said before, hardware wallets, such as Ledger or Trezor, offer offline storage and enhanced protection against hacking attempts. Software wallets, mobile wallets, or web wallets should be secured with strong passwords, backup phrases, and regular updates to mitigate potential vulnerabilities.

Be cautious when providing personal information to exchanges or third-party platforms. Ensure the platforms you use employ robust data protection measures and adhere to privacy regulations. Avoid sharing sensitive information on unsecured websites or platforms with questionable security practices.

Beware of phishing attempts and scams. Exercise caution when clicking on links, downloading software, or sharing sensitive information. Be vigilant about verifying the authenticity of websites, emails, and communication channels to avoid falling victim to fraudulent schemes.

Moreover, stay informed about the latest security practices and updates within the cryptocurrency community. Keep your wallets, software, and devices updated with the latest security patches to protect against potential vulnerabilities. Follow best practices such as using unique and strong passwords, enabling 2FA, and avoiding public Wi-Fi networks for sensitive transactions.

The long and short of it is: Buying and selling cryptocurrency involves navigating various payment methods and understanding essential security considerations. Whether using fiat currency, engaging in peer-to-peer transactions, or leveraging cryptocurrency-to-cryptocurrency exchanges, individuals must prioritize security by choosing reputable platforms, securing wallets, protecting personal information, and staying vigilant against phishing attempts and scams. By following these guidelines, users can confidently participate in the cryptocurrency market while safeguarding their assets and personal information.

Understanding Market Trends and Making Informed Buying/Selling Decisions

Cryptocurrencies have gained significant attention in recent years, attracting both investors and traders looking to capitalize on their potential. However, the cryptocurrency market is highly volatile and influenced by various factors. Understanding market trends and making informed buying and selling decisions are crucial to navigating this dynamic landscape successfully. As a result, it might be wise for us to explore the importance of market trends, key indicators for analysis, and strategies for making informed decisions when buying or selling cryptocurrencies.

First, let's start with an axiom: the cryptocurrency market is known for its volatility, with prices fluctuating rapidly. Studying market trends is useful to help identify patterns and price movements, enabling traders to seize opportunities and mitigate risks.

In a digression, it might be added that Italian economist Vilfredo Pareto (1848 – 1923) was one of the earliest people to notice that the economy was driven not by cold, clinical logic, but by the irrational impulses of human beings. Market trends, he asserted, reflect the collective sentiment and behavior of market participants. Understanding trends provides insights into market psychology, helping traders gauge market sentiment and make informed decisions based on prevailing market conditions.

It's important for you to establish some key indicators for analysis. For instance, there's technical analysis, which involves applying scrutiny to historical price and volume data to identify patterns, trends, and support/resistance levels. Common technical analysis tools include trend lines, moving averages, and oscillators like Relative Strength Index (RSI) and Moving Average Convergence Divergence (MACD).

TradingView, Coinigy, CoinGecko and BinanceTradingView are just a few of the platforms that will help you crunch the numbers, see the trendlines and show the charts of historical data.

Aside from "technical analysis," there's also fundamental analysis. This focuses on evaluating the underlying factors that can impact the value of cryptocurrencies. This includes assessing the project's technology, team, partnerships, market adoption, and regulatory developments. Fundamental analysis helps identify the intrinsic value and long-term potential of a cryptocurrency.

In addition to fundamental analysis is something

called "sentiment analysis". This procedure involves gauging market sentiment through social media, news sentiment, and other sentiment indicators. This analysis provides insights into the overall mood of the market, which can influence buying and selling decisions. Santiment, LunarCrush, the Tie and Predicoin are a few websites that offer sentiment analysis.

Once you've created a comprehensive strategy for analyzing the market, now's the time to think about strategies for making informed buying and selling decisions. This starts with setting clear goals and taking into account risk management protocols. Before entering the market, establish clear objectives and risk tolerance levels. Define your investment intentions, time horizon, and acceptable level of risk. Implement risk mitigation techniques such as setting stop-loss orders or diversifying your portfolio to manage potential losses.

Then create a trading plan. Develop a well-defined trading strategy that outlines your entry and exit strategies, risk-reward ratios, and position sizing. Stick to your plan, avoid emotional decisions, and review and adjust your plan as market conditions evolve.

But don't be entirely insensitive to outside feedback. Stay informed about industry news, regulatory changes, and market developments. Follow reputable cryptocurrency news sources, participate in relevant communities, and consider joining discussion forums to gain insights and stay updated with the latest information.

Also, don't forget to implement stop-loss and take-profit orders to help limit losses and secure profits automatically. Stop-loss orders trigger a sell order if the price reaches a predetermined level, protecting against significant losses. Take-profit orders automatically sell when the price reaches a specified target, securing gains.

Likewise, think about dollar-cost averaging. This involves regularly investing a fixed amount into a particular cryptocurrency, regardless of its price. This strategy reduces the impact of short-term price fluctuations, allows for disciplined investing, and averages out the purchase price over time.

Part of risk mitigation includes diversifying your cryptocurrency portfolio across different cryptocurrencies, sectors, and asset classes. This spreads risk and minimizes exposure to the volatility of individual cryptocurrencies.

Avoid what's called FOMO (Fear of Missing Out) and panic selling. These can lead to impulsive and emotionally-driven decisions. Develop discipline and avoid making decisions solely based on short-term market fluctuations or peer-pressure.

The cryptocurrency market is ever-evolving, and trends can change rapidly. Stay curious, continuously learn, adapt your strategies as needed, and refine your understanding of market dynamics to make informed decisions.

Conclusion

Understanding market trends and making informed buying/selling decisions are critical for navigating the dynamic cryptocurrency market. By analyzing key indicators through technical, fundamental, and sentiment analysis, traders can gain insights into market trends and sentiment. Implementing strategies such as setting goals, risk management, creating a trading plan, and staying informed about news and market developments empowers investors to make informed decisions. Additionally, mitigating risks, controlling emotions, and continuously learning contribute to building a solid foundation for successful cryptocurrency investing. Remember that the cryptocurrency market carries inherent risks, and thorough research, due diligence, and a disciplined approach are essential for making informed decisions and achieving long-term investment goals.

Chapter Six
Storing and Securing Cryptocurrency

A s the popularity of cryptocurrencies continues to rise, the need for secure storage solutions has become paramount. Cryptocurrency holders must protect their digital assets from theft and unauthorized access. So, even though we've already lightly touched upon some of these topics, it might bear repeating certain things. (After all, in the world of cryptocurrency, you'll encounter the word *hash* a lot—such as "hash code," "hash value," "hash function," etc. So we might as well rehash.) Firstly, let's circle back to hot wallets. Just to repeat: Hot wallets are digital wallets connected to the internet and accessible through software applications or online platforms. They are commonly used for everyday transactions and quick access to cryptocurrencies. Some key aspects of hot wallets are:

a. Accessibility and Convenience: Hot wallets provide instant access to cryptocurrencies from various devices such as smartphones, tablets, or computers. They are user-friendly and suitable for frequent transactions.

b. Online Security Risks: Hot wallets pose a higher security risk due to their constant connection to the internet. They are susceptible to hacking, malware, and phishing attacks. Users must employ robust security practices like two-factor authentication (2FA) and regularly update software to mitigate these risks.

c. Types of Hot Wallets: Web wallets, mobile wallets, and software wallets are common types of hot wallets. Web wallets are accessed through browsers, mobile wallets through smartphone apps, and software wallets through desktop applications.

Next, we have so-called cold wallets: Also known as offline wallets, these store cryptocurrencies offline, disconnected from the internet. They offer enhanced security by reducing the risk of online attacks. Let's explore their main characteristics:

a. Security Benefits: Cold wallets provide a higher level of security as they are not constantly connected to the internet. This minimizes the risk of hacking, malware, and phishing attacks. Cold wallets are suitable for long-term storage and large cryptocurrency holdings.

b. Types of Cold Wallets: Paper wallets and hardware wallets are common types of cold wallets. Paper wallets involve generating a public and private key pair on a secure offline device and printing them on paper. Hardware wallets, discussed further below, provide an additional layer of security with dedicated secure hardware devices.

c. Trade-Off: While cold wallets offer enhanced security, they can be less convenient for frequent transactions. Users need to transfer funds from a cold wallet to a hot wallet or an exchange to facilitate transactions.

In contrast to the foregoing are hardware wallets: Hardware wallets are physical devices designed specifically for storing cryptocurrencies securely. They combine the convenience of hot wallets with the enhanced security of cold wallets. Here's what you need to know about hardware wallets:

a. Dedicated Security: Hardware wallets offer robust security features, including secure microcontrollers, encryption, PIN protection, and built-in screens for verifying transactions. Private keys remain stored securely on the device, minimizing the risk of exposure.

b. Offline Storage: Hardware wallets store private keys offline, preventing them from being exposed to potential online threats. The device is only connected to the internet when initiating transactions, reducing the risk of unauthorized access.

c. User-Friendly Experience: Hardware wallets provide a user-friendly interface for managing and accessing cryptocurrencies. They often come with companion software applications that enable users to easily initiate transactions and manage their assets.

d. Cost Considerations: Hardware wallets are typically priced higher than software wallets or even cold storage alternatives. However, their enhanced security features and peace of mind make them a worthwhile investment for

individuals   holding   significant
cryptocurrency assets.

Now that you understand the basics, it's time to choose the right storage option. When selecting a storage option for cryptocurrencies, several factors should be considered. The principal consideration should be to assess the security features and vulnerabilities associated with each storage option. Consider your risk tolerance and the value of the cryptocurrencies you hold.

Determine how frequently you need to access your cryptocurrencies. If you engage in frequent transactions, a hot wallet might be more suitable. For long-term storage, a cold wallet or hardware wallet offers greater security.

Balance the convenience of accessing cryptocurrencies quickly with the security risks involved. Hot wallets provide convenience but come with a higher risk profile. Cold wallets and hardware wallets prioritize security but may be less convenient for everyday use.

Consider the backup and recovery mechanisms offered by the storage option. Ensure you have a reliable backup plan for your private keys to avoid the risk of losing access to your cryptocurrencies.

We'll draw this section to a close by saying: Choosing the right storage option for cryptocurrencies is crucial for ensuring the security and accessibility of your digital assets. Hot wallets provide convenience but require careful security measures. Cold wallets, such as paper wallets, offer enhanced security through offline storage, while hardware wallets combine security and user-friendliness. Assess your needs, risk tolerance, and the value of your holdings to determine the most appropriate storage option. Remember to regularly update your software, use strong passwords and 2FA, and remain vigilant against potential threats. By implementing proper security measures and selecting the right storage option, you can safeguard your cryptocurrencies and have peace of mind in this digital asset ecosystem.

Implementing Security Measures to Protect Cryptocurrency Investments

The rise of cryptocurrencies has brought about numerous opportunities for investment and wealth creation. However, the decentralized nature of cryptocurrencies and the potential for cyber threats necessitate robust security measures to protect one's cryptocurrency investments. As a result, we'll stop a moment to consider various security measures that can be implemented to safeguard cryptocurrency holdings, including securing wallets, practicing strong password hygiene, utilizing two-factor authentication (2FA), adopting hardware wallets, and employing vigilance against phishing attacks.

With respect to securing wallets . . . we'll start with users employing hot wallets. It's essential to keep software and applications up-to-date with the latest security patches. Regularly backing up wallet files and encrypting private keys are vital to protect against data loss and unauthorized access.

Regarding cold wallets (such as hardware wallets or paper wallets), these provide enhanced security by keeping private keys offline. Users must store these wallets in secure physical locations, protect them from damage, and ensure they are inaccessible to unauthorized individuals.

Next, take a moment to think about strong password hygiene. Using strong, complex, and unique passwords for cryptocurrency accounts is crucial. Avoid common passwords, and consider utilizing a password manager to generate and securely store passwords.

Enable Multi-Factor Authentication (2FA) for cryptocurrency wallets and exchanges whenever possible. 2FA adds an additional layer of security by requiring a second verification factor, such as a code from a mobile app or a text message, to access an account.

Hardware Wallets: Hardware wallets, such as Ledger Nano X or KeepKey, offer offline storage and enhanced security for cryptocurrency investments. These devices store private keys securely and require physical authentication, making them less vulnerable to hacking or malware attacks.

Another consideration to harden your defenses against are phishing attacks. (A phishing attack is a type of cybercrime where criminals impersonate a legitimate individual, organization, or company to trick individuals into revealing sensitive information, such as usernames, passwords, credit card details, or cryptocurrency wallet credentials. The attackers typically use deceptive tactics, such as fraudulent emails, websites, or messages, to deceive victims into believing they are interacting with a trusted entity.) Phishing scams are prevalent in the cryptocurrency space. To protect investments, users must remain vigilant and employ the following measures:

1. Verifying Website Authenticity: Always ensure you are accessing legitimate cryptocurrency exchange or wallet websites by double-checking the URL, examining security indicators (e.g., SSL certificates), and avoiding clicking on suspicious links.

2. Avoiding Suspicious Emails and Messages: Be cautious of unsolicited emails or messages that ask for personal information or request urgent actions. Legitimate service providers typically do not ask for sensitive data via email.

3. Secure Communication Channels: When communicating with cryptocurrency exchanges or support teams, ensure you are using secure communication channels such as encrypted messaging platforms or secure email services.

All of this is meaningless, of course, if you don't practice basic internet security. Make sure you have a secure network connection. Avoid using public Wi-Fi networks when accessing cryptocurrency wallets or exchanges. Public networks are often unsecured and vulnerable to eavesdropping or man-in-the-middle attacks.

Furthermore, keep all devices, including computers and smartphones, up to date with the latest operating system updates and security patches. Regular updates help protect against known vulnerabilities.

Install reputable antivirus software and enable firewalls on devices used for cryptocurrency transactions. These security measures provide an additional layer of protection against malware and unauthorized access.

Regularly back up wallet files and store backup copies in secure locations. It is essential to follow the backup instructions specific to the wallet or exchange being used. Test the restoration process periodically to ensure backups are functional.

Stay informed about the latest security practices, vulnerabilities, and scams within the cryptocurrency community. Regularly review security guidelines and best practices provided by cryptocurrency wallets, exchanges, and industry experts.

Implementing robust security measures is paramount to protecting cryptocurrency investments. Safeguarding wallets, using strong passwords and 2FA, adopting hardware wallets, and remaining vigilant against phishing attacks are vital steps to ensure the security of digital assets. Additionally, practicing secure internet practices, keeping devices up to date, and maintaining backups contribute to a comprehensive security strategy. The evolving nature of cyber threats demands ongoing education and awareness. By implementing these security measures and staying informed about emerging threats, cryptocurrency investors can significantly reduce the risks associated with holding and transacting cryptocurrencies, providing peace of mind and protecting their investments for the long term.

Safeguarding Against Scams and Other Risks

As the popularity of cryptocurrencies continues to grow, so does the prevalence of scams, phishing attempts, and other risks targeting cryptocurrency investors. Safeguarding cryptocurrency investments is essential to protect against financial loss and maintain the integrity of digital assets.

Number one: Be proactive. Before investing in a cryptocurrency project or platform, conduct thorough research to understand its purpose, technology, team, community, and overall credibility. Scrutinize the project's whitepaper, website, and social media channels to gain insights into its legitimacy and potential risks.

Consider the regulatory landscape surrounding the cryptocurrency project or platform. Understanding the legal framework, compliance requirements, and regulatory oversight can help mitigate risks associated with potential legal and regulatory challenges.

Pay attention to red flags. Be wary of investment opportunities or projects that promise unrealistic returns or make exaggerated claims. If an investment opportunity appears too good to be true, it likely is.

Transparency is crucial in the cryptocurrency space.

CRYPTOCURRENCY FOR SENIORS

If a project or platform lacks transparency regarding its technology, team, or financials, it raises concerns. Look for projects with clear communication and a track record of transparency.

Verify information from multiple reputable sources to avoid falling victim to misinformation or scams. Rely on trusted cryptocurrency news outlets, credible industry experts, and official project communications.

Be cautious of unsolicited emails or messages that request personal information, private keys, or immediate action.

Verify the authenticity of websites, links, and communication channels before sharing personal information or entering login credentials. Check for secure connections (HTTPS) and examine website URLs for any discrepancies or misspellings.

Regularly assess and monitor investments for any suspicious activities, market volatility, or emerging risks. Stay informed about market trends, regulatory changes, and potential security vulnerabilities.

Stay informed about the latest security practices, emerging scams, and phishing techniques prevalent in the cryptocurrency space. Educate yourself on the fundamentals of cryptocurrencies, blockchain technology, and security best practices.

If you're uncertain as to what to do, don't be afraid to engage professional services, such as cybersecurity firms or legal advisors specializing in cryptocurrencies. These experts can provide valuable insights, conduct security audits, and help navigate complex regulatory landscapes.

Conclusion

Safeguarding cryptocurrency investments against scams, phishing attempts, and other risks requires a proactive and informed approach. By conducting thorough research, identifying red flags, securing digital wallets, recognizing phishing attempts, and maintaining a proactive risk management strategy, investors can minimize the risks associated with cryptocurrency investments. Staying informed, adopting best practices, and remaining vigilant are essential to protect against financial loss and maintain the integrity of cryptocurrency investments. As the cryptocurrency ecosystem evolves, continuous education and adaptation to emerging risks are crucial to ensure the long-term security and success of cryptocurrency investments.

Chapter Seven

Using Cryptocurrency in Everyday Life

Cryptocurrency has emerged as a transformative force in the realm of digital finance, offering individuals a decentralized and secure method of conducting online transactions. While initially popularized as an investment asset, cryptocurrencies are increasingly being used to buy things online. It might be good, therefore, to explore the process of using cryptocurrency for online purchases, covering key aspects such as setting up a digital wallet, selecting compatible merchants, understanding payment gateways, considering transaction fees, and addressing potential challenges.

Understanding How to Use Cryptocurrency for Online Purchases

As we already discussed, it will be necessary to set up a cryptocurrency wallet. You already know the selection: there are software wallets (desktop, mobile, or web-based), hardware wallets, and paper wallets. Each type has its own pros and cons in terms of accessibility and security.

Install the chosen wallet software and follow the setup instructions. Implement necessary security measures, such as setting strong passwords, enabling two-factor authentication (2FA), and storing backup phrases or private keys securely. These precautions protect your funds from unauthorized access.

Next, you have to locate merchants that accept cryptocurrencies. Likewise, explore payment processors that facilitate cryptocurrency transactions for vendors. Platforms like BitPay, CoinGate, and Coinbase Commerce enable merchants to accept cryptocurrencies as payment. Look for merchants that integrate these payment processors into their checkout systems.

(There are some banks and financial institutions that offer debit cards that are directly linked to your cryptocurrency wallet. These cards are associated with specific cryptocurrencies like Bitcoin or Ethereum and allow users to convert their digital assets into fiat currencies at the time of purchase.)

Some merchants directly accept cryptocurrencies as payment without using payment processors. Look for "Bitcoin Accepted Here" or similar signs on merchant websites or inquire about cryptocurrency payment options before making a purchase.

There are also things known as "payment gateways". Payment gateways act as intermediaries between customers, merchants, and cryptocurrency networks. They facilitate the smooth processing of cryptocurrency transactions, ensuring the accuracy and security of payments. Familiarize yourself with popular payment gateway options, such as CoinGate, Coinify, and CoinPayments.

If a merchant only accepts fiat currencies, you may need to convert your cryptocurrencies to traditional currencies. Exchanges like Coinbase, Kraken, and

Binance provide options to convert cryptocurrencies into fiat currencies, allowing you to make purchases with merchants that do not directly accept cryptocurrencies.

Cryptocurrency transactions involve blockchain fees to incentivize miners and validate transactions. The fees vary depending on network congestion and transaction priority. Before making a purchase, consider the current fee structure and ensure you have adequate funds to cover the transaction fees.

Payment processors may charge fees for facilitating cryptocurrency transactions. Research and compare the fees associated with different payment processors to ensure they align with your budget and transaction volume.

Despite the increasing convenience, there *are* some potential challenges. Cryptocurrencies are known for their price volatility. Consider the potential price fluctuations when making a purchase, especially for larger or time-sensitive transactions. Strategies like converting cryptocurrencies to stablecoins or utilizing merchant services that instantly convert cryptocurrencies into fiat currencies can mitigate this risk.

While cryptocurrency acceptance is growing, it is not yet universal. Not all merchants accept cryptocurrencies, so it is important to verify the payment options before initiating a purchase. Explore merchant directories like Coinmap or websites dedicated to listing crypto-accepting merchants.

Regarding refunds and disputes, cryptocurrency

transactions are typically irreversible. In cases where refunds or disputes arise, resolving issues can be more challenging than traditional payment methods. Ensure clear communication with the merchant regarding refund policies and consider purchasing from reputable vendors.

Let us draw this section to a successful conclusion by saying: cryptocurrency for online purchases offers a secure, efficient, and decentralized alternative to traditional payment methods. By setting up a cryptocurrency wallet, finding merchants that accept cryptocurrencies, understanding payment gateways, considering transaction fees, and addressing potential challenges, individuals can confidently navigate the process of using cryptocurrencies for online purchases. As the adoption of cryptocurrencies continues to grow, more merchants are likely to accept digital currencies, providing greater convenience and accessibility for consumers. Embracing this emerging payment method empowers individuals to fully leverage the advantages of cryptocurrencies in their day-to-day transactions.

Exploring Businesses and Platforms that Accept Cryptocurrency Payments

The adoption of cryptocurrencies as a form of payment has witnessed significant growth over the past decade. As digital currencies gain mainstream recognition, an increasing number of businesses and platforms are embracing this transformative technology. Consider E-commerce, for starters.

CRYPTOCURRENCY FOR SENIORS

Cryptocurrencies offer numerous benefits for e-commerce businesses, such as offering global reach. Cryptocurrencies transcend geographical borders, enabling e-commerce businesses to tap into a global customer-base without the limitations of traditional banking systems or exchange rates.

Cryptocurrency transactions also often involve lower fees compared to traditional payment methods, allowing businesses to increase their profit margins and offer competitive pricing.

In addition, they provide an added layer of security, reducing the risk of fraud and chargebacks. The use of blockchain technology ensures transparency and immutability, enhancing trust between merchants and consumers.

Another sector opening up to cryptocurrencies is the hospitality industry. They're increasingly accepting cryptocurrency payments, offering advantages, such as seamless cross-border transactions. Cryptocurrencies eliminate the need for currency-conversions and traditional banking intermediaries, making international transactions more efficient and cost-effective.

Furthermore, cryptocurrency payments provide travelers with increased privacy, reducing the need to disclose sensitive personal information during the booking process.

The food and beverage industry is coming along, too. Cryptocurrency-adoption in the food and beverage sector offers several benefits: They facilitate quick and secure transactions, minimizing waiting times for both customers and merchants. Some food and beverage establishments offer loyalty programs based on cryptocurrencies, providing incentives for customers to patronize their establishments.

Another beneficial featured opened up to someone using cryptos is the ability to do microtransactions. Cryptocurrencies make it convenient for customers to pay for small purchases or order food online without the need for traditional payment methods.

By the way, don't forget about how cryptocurrencies have made a significant impact on the philanthropy sector, providing the following advantages:

1. Transparency and Accountability: Cryptocurrency donations can be tracked on the blockchain, ensuring transparency and accountability in charitable transactions. Donors can verify the allocation of funds, fostering trust in charitable organizations.

2. Reduced Transaction Costs: Cryptocurrency donations often involve lower transaction fees, ensuring that a greater portion of donated funds directly reaches the intended beneficiaries.

3. Global Donor Base: Cryptocurrencies enable charitable organizations to receive donations from around the world, eliminating barriers such as international banking fees and exchange rate fluctuations.

And, of course, there are other industries adopting the new technology—like gaming and online services, retail, real estate, education, and so forth.

Even the publishing industry is getting in on the act, leveraging cryptocurrencies to provide a seamless method for recurring payments and subscription-based services, eliminating the need for regular credit card updates or manual transactions.

To distill it down into the simplest possible terms: The acceptance of cryptocurrency payments by businesses and platforms has expanded across various sectors, bringing about numerous advantages for merchants and consumers alike. Across the full panoply of the economy, cryptocurrencies have disrupted traditional payment systems, offering global accessibility, lower transaction fees, enhanced security, and increased privacy. The growing adoption of cryptocurrencies in everyday transactions not only demonstrates the evolution of digital currencies but also presents opportunities for financial inclusion and economic empowerment. As cryptocurrency acceptance continues to expand, businesses and consumers stand to benefit from the advantages provided by this transformative technology, reshaping the way we perceive and engage in financial transactions.

Discussing the Benefits and Challenges of Using Cryptocurrency in Daily Transactions

There are both benefits *and* challenges to using cryptocurrency in daily transactions. On the positive side of the balance sheet, the new technology offers such advantages as decentralization, security, and financial inclusion; while, on the other side of the balance sheet, there are concerns such as price volatility, regulatory uncertainty, and adoption-barriers. Understanding the implications of cryptocurrency in daily transactions empowers individuals to navigate this evolving landscape effectively.

First, let's start with the benefits. Cryptocurrencies operate on decentralized networks, allowing individuals to have direct control over their finances. This eliminates the need for intermediaries such as banks, empowering users with financial autonomy and freedom.

In addition, cryptocurrency transactions are secured through cryptographic algorithms, ensuring the integrity and confidentiality of financial data. Blockchain technology enables transparent and immutable transactions, reducing the risk of fraud, identity theft, and unauthorized access.

Cryptocurrency transactions often involve lower fees compared to traditional payment methods. By eliminating intermediaries, such as banks or payment processors, individuals can save on transaction fees, particularly for cross-border transactions.

Cryptocurrencies transcend geographical boundaries, providing access to financial services for the unbanked and underbanked populations. It enables individuals without traditional banking infrastructure to participate in the global economy and access digital financial services.

Despite all these good aspects, there is still the issue of price volatility. Cryptocurrencies are known for their price volatility, which can present challenges for daily transactions. The value of cryptocurrencies can fluctuate significantly in short periods, making it difficult to ascertain the accurate purchasing power and pricing stability.

Furthermore, cryptocurrency regulations vary across jurisdictions, leading to uncertainty and potential legal barriers. The lack of consistent and comprehensive regulations can impact the acceptance and usability of cryptocurrencies in daily transactions.

Widespread adoption of cryptocurrencies in daily transactions is hindered by various factors, including limited merchant acceptance, lack of user-friendly interfaces, and technical complexities. Overcoming these barriers requires increased awareness, user education, and improved infrastructure.

As cryptocurrency networks grow, scalability and transaction speed become significant challenges. Blockchain networks like Bitcoin and Ethereum may experience congestion during periods of high demand, leading to slower transaction processing times.

Of course, you can overcome the challenges and offset the liabilities by enhancing your education and awareness. This will be crucial for widespread adoption. Promoting the understanding of cryptocurrency fundamentals, security practices, and the benefits it offers can alleviate concerns and drive acceptance.

Continued technological advancements, such as the development of scalable blockchain solutions and user-friendly interfaces, can address scalability and usability challenges, making daily transactions more efficient and convenient.

Establishing clear and comprehensive regulatory frameworks can provide certainty and foster trust within the cryptocurrency ecosystem. Balanced regulations that protect consumers, prevent fraud, and promote innovation are essential for wider adoption.

Encouraging more businesses to accept cryptocurrencies as payment can increase their utility in daily transactions. Initiatives to incentivize and educate merchants on the benefits of cryptocurrency acceptance can drive adoption and create a positive feedback loop.

Conclusion

The use of cryptocurrency in daily transactions offers numerous benefits, including decentralization, enhanced security, reduced transaction costs, and global accessibility. However, challenges such as price volatility, regulatory uncertainty, adoption barriers, and scalability concerns must be addressed for widespread acceptance. Overcoming these challenges requires collective efforts from individuals, businesses, and regulators. By fostering education, technological advancements, regulatory clarity, and increased merchant adoption, cryptocurrencies can become a mainstream form of transaction in daily life.

CRYPTOCURRENCY FOR SENIORS

Embracing the benefits of cryptocurrency in daily transactions enables individuals to experience greater financial control, security, and inclusivity in the evolving digital economy.

Chapter Eight

Taxation and Legal Considerations

The rise of cryptocurrencies has brought forth a complex intersection between digital assets and traditional tax frameworks. As governments worldwide grapple with how to classify and regulate cryptocurrencies, understanding the taxation and legal ramifications is crucial for individuals and businesses involved in cryptocurrency transactions. It might be time, therefore, to examine the current landscape of cryptocurrency taxation, including regulatory approaches, reporting obligations, capital gains, and legal considerations.

Understanding the Tax Implications of Owning and Trading Cryptocurrencies

As cryptocurrencies become more mainstream, it is essential to comprehend the tax implications associated with owning and trading these digital assets. Tax authorities often classify cryptocurrencies as assets, commodities, or currencies, which impacts their tax treatment. Determining the classification helps identify the applicable tax regulations and reporting obligations.

Profits from the sale or exchange of cryptocurrencies are typically subject to capital gains tax. The tax liability is calculated based on the difference between the purchase price and the selling price of the cryptocurrencies.

Tax rates for capital gains can vary based on the length of time the cryptocurrencies were held. Short-term holdings may attract higher tax rates compared to long-term holdings.

Many tax authorities require individuals to report transactions, including buying, selling, and exchanging cryptocurrencies. The reporting may involve details such as transaction dates, values in fiat currency, and the purpose of the transaction.

Individuals engaged in cryptocurrency mining, staking, or receiving income in cryptocurrencies must report such earnings as taxable income. This includes freelance work, cryptocurrency rewards, or payments received in cryptocurrencies.

Understanding the tax obligations associated with cryptocurrency activities allows individuals to plan and manage their tax liabilities effectively. Seeking professional advice can help identify tax planning strategies and optimize tax positions.

Calculating the cost-basis of cryptocurrencies is crucial for accurate tax reporting. Different methods, such as First-In-First-Out (FIFO) or Specific Identification, can be used to determine the cost basis of cryptocurrencies acquired and sold.

Individuals engaged in cryptocurrency mining or trading may be eligible for deductions related to business expenses. These deductions can include electricity costs, hardware expenses, and other operational outlays.

Cryptocurrency taxation varies across jurisdictions, with countries adopting different approaches. Some countries treat cryptocurrencies as assets subject to capital gains tax, while others view them as currency or commodities. Understanding the tax regulations in the relevant jurisdiction is crucial for compliance. Cryptocurrency investors engaged in cross-border transactions may face challenges related to double taxation. Tax treaties between countries can help mitigate double taxation by providing mechanisms for credits or exemptions.

International cryptocurrency transactions may require compliance with additional reporting obligations, such as the Foreign Account Tax Compliance Act (FATCA) or Common Reporting Standards (CRS). It is important to understand these requirements and ensure compliance to avoid penalties and legal issues.

Tax regulations for cryptocurrencies are evolving as governments seek to address the challenges posed by these digital assets. Regular updates and clarifications are expected as tax authorities respond to the changing landscape of cryptocurrencies.

Blockchain technology and distributed ledger systems offer opportunities to enhance tax reporting and compliance. Innovations such as transparent and immutable transaction records can simplify tax reporting processes.

As governments focus on cryptocurrency activities, increased scrutiny and audits may occur to ensure compliance with tax regulations. Maintaining accurate records and staying abreast of reporting requirements is crucial to navigate potential audits.

To recap: Understanding the tax implications of owning and trading cryptocurrencies is paramount for individuals involved in cryptocurrency activities. The tax treatment of cryptocurrencies varies across jurisdictions, with considerations such as capital gains tax, reporting obligations, and tax planning strategies playing vital roles. International perspectives add an additional layer of complexity, requiring compliance with varying tax regulations and reporting obligations. As new developments occur and regulatory frameworks mature, staying informed about tax obligations and seeking professional advice are essential to ensure compliance and effectively manage tax liabilities. By embracing the tax considerations associated with cryptocurrencies, individuals can navigate the evolving tax landscape and foster a responsible and transparent cryptocurrency ecosystem.

Navigating Legal Regulations and Reporting Requirements

The emergence of cryptocurrencies has brought about a unique set of legal and regulatory challenges for individuals and businesses operating within this rapidly evolving landscape. By understanding the regulations in their jurisdiction, individuals and businesses can navigate the legal framework surrounding cryptocurrencies and ensure compliance with reporting obligations.

As just alluded to a few pages ago, countries have

adopted different regulatory approaches toward cryptocurrencies. Some jurisdictions embrace cryptocurrencies (such as El Salvador which, in 2021, became the first country to adopt Bitcoin as an official currency), while others are cautious, imposing stringent regulations or outright bans (like Saudi Arabia).

Most governments seek to achieve various objectives with cryptocurrency regulations, such as protecting consumers, preventing illicit activities like money laundering and terrorism financing, and promoting market integrity.

Cryptocurrency businesses must consider legal structures suitable for their operations, such as forming corporations, partnerships, or limited liability companies (LLCs). These structures determine legal liability, tax obligations, and regulatory compliance requirements.

Certain jurisdictions require cryptocurrency businesses, such as exchanges or custodial service providers, to obtain licenses or register with relevant regulatory authorities. Compliance with anti-money laundering (AML) and know-your-customer (KYC) regulations is often a prerequisite.

Cryptocurrency businesses must also abide by consumer protection laws, ensuring transparency, disclosure, and fair practices. Measures such as secure custody of customer funds and protection against fraud are vital for maintaining trust and legal compliance.

Individuals engaged in cryptocurrency activities, such

as mining or receiving income in cryptocurrencies, must report and pay taxes on these earnings. The tax treatment varies across jurisdictions. For instance, The Internal Revenue Service (IRS) in the United States treats cryptocurrencies as property rather than currency. Japan and Switzerland, by contrast, see it as legal tender.

Profits from the sale or exchange of cryptocurrencies are typically subject to capital gains tax. Tax authorities require individuals to report the gains and losses associated with cryptocurrency transactions, and applicable tax-rates depend on factors such as the holding-period and the individual's tax bracket.

Then there's, of course, the Value-Added Tax (VAT) and Goods and Services Tax (GST). The VAT/GST treatment of cryptocurrencies varies between jurisdictions. Some countries exempt cryptocurrency transactions from VAT/GST, while others consider them taxable supplies. Understanding the specific rules in each jurisdiction is crucial for compliance.

Individuals engaging in cryptocurrency transactions may have reporting obligations, such as disclosing the details of the transactions, including dates, values, and counterparties. These requirements are aimed at preventing money laundering, tax evasion, and other illicit activities. Cryptocurrency users with offshore accounts or holdings may have additional reporting obligations, such as reporting foreign financial accounts or complying with the Foreign Account Tax Compliance Act (FATCA) requirements. Failure to comply with these obligations can result in penalties and legal consequences.

Staying informed about the legal regulations governing cryptocurrencies is essential. Routinely monitoring updates from regulatory authorities and seeking legal advice can help individuals and businesses navigate the evolving legal landscape effectively. Implementing robust compliance measures, such as KYC/AML procedures, secure custody solutions, and adequate record-keeping practices, demonstrates a commitment to statutory compliance and helps mitigate legal risks.

Engaging with regulatory authorities and participating in public consultations or industry working groups can contribute to the development of balanced and effective regulations. It fosters an open dialogue between stakeholders and regulatory bodies, facilitating responsible innovation and regulatory clarity.

Cryptocurrency regulations are still evolving as governments strive to keep pace with technological advancements. Future developments may include enhanced regulatory frameworks, standardized reporting requirements, and increased international collaboration.

With cryptocurrencies operating on a global scale, cross-border transactions pose unique challenges. Cooperation between jurisdictions and the development of consistent international frameworks can streamline reporting requirements and address regulatory concerns.

Emerging technologies such as blockchain analytics

and monitoring tools are being developed to assist with compliance and reporting obligations. These tools can provide transparency, traceability, and real-time reporting capabilities to enhance regulatory compliance.

In short, navigating the legal regulations and reporting requirements associated with cryptocurrencies is crucial for individuals and businesses operating in this dynamic landscape. Understanding the regulatory approaches, legal considerations, and tax implications of cryptocurrencies enables compliance with reporting obligations and mitigates legal risks. As the cryptocurrency ecosystem continues to evolve, staying informed about regulatory developments, seeking legal advice, and implementing robust compliance measures are essential for individuals and businesses to operate within the bounds of the law. By embracing responsible practices and engaging with regulatory authorities, the cryptocurrency community can contribute to the development of balanced and effective regulatory frameworks that foster innovation while addressing legitimate concerns.

Seeking Professional Advice for Tax Planning and Compliance

As cryptocurrencies gain prominence in the world of finance, individuals and businesses engaged in cryptocurrency activities face complex tax planning and compliance challenges. Navigating the ever-evolving tax regulations and reporting obligations associated with cryptocurrencies can be daunting without proper expertise.

Cryptocurrency taxation regulations are continually evolving as governments seek to address the unique features and challenges posed by digital assets. Changes in laws, interpretations, and guidance can significantly impact tax obligations and reporting requirements.

As aforementioned, cryptocurrencies are treated differently in various jurisdictions, with variations in their classification as currency, property, commodity, or security. These classifications determine the specific tax rules and implications that apply.

There are some websites you can consult, such as:

1. CoinTracker (cointracker.io): CoinTracker provides tax software and resources for cryptocurrency users. They offer a blog section that covers various tax-related topics and regularly updates users on changes in tax regulations and reporting requirements.

2. CryptoTaxGuide (cryptotaxguide.io): CryptoTaxGuide is a comprehensive resource for cryptocurrency tax information. They provide guides, articles, and FAQs to help users understand tax obligations and reporting requirements specific to their jurisdiction.

3. CryptoTrader.Tax (cryptotrader.tax): CryptoTrader.Tax offers tax reporting software and resources for cryptocurrency investors and traders. Their website provides information on tax laws and guidelines in

different countries, along with tax calculators and tax reporting tools.

4. Internal Revenue Service (IRS) (irs.gov): The official website of the U.S. Internal Revenue Service provides resources and publications on cryptocurrency taxation. The IRS regularly updates its guidance on cryptocurrency tax treatment, providing valuable information for U.S. taxpayers.

5. Taxation and Customs Union - European Commission (ec.europa.eu/taxation_customs): The European Commission's website on taxation and customs provides information on tax regulations and guidance within the European Union. Users can access country-specific tax guidelines and resources related to cryptocurrencies.

6. HM Revenue & Customs (HMRC) (gov.uk/government/organisations/hm-revenue-customs): HMRC's website offers guidance on cryptocurrency tax treatment in the United Kingdom. It provides information on tax obligations, reporting requirements, and relevant resources for taxpayers.

7. Australian Taxation Office (ATO) (ato.gov.au): The ATO website offers guidance on cryptocurrency taxation in Australia. It provides information on tax treatment, record-keeping requirements, and tax implications for individuals and

> businesses engaged in cryptocurrency activities.

These are just a few of the resources available. But no website or software package is a substitute for tax professionals with expertise in cryptocurrency. They possess the necessary knowledge and experience to navigate the complexities of this emerging field. They stay updated with the latest developments, regulations, and best practices, ensuring accurate tax planning and compliance.

Professional advice ensures that cryptocurrencies are appropriately classified and reported for tax purposes. This includes distinguishing between personal use, investment, and business activities, as well as reporting requirements for mining, staking, and income received in cryptocurrencies. Tax professionals can help individuals optimize their tax positions by identifying potential deductions, allowances, and tax credits available for cryptocurrency activities. They can provide insights into tax-efficient strategies for buying, selling, and holding cryptocurrencies. In addition, tax professionals can assist in tracking and reporting cryptocurrency transactions accurately. They ensure compliance with reporting obligations, including the disclosure of transaction details, counterparties, and values in fiat currency, as required by tax authorities.

Cryptocurrency activities with an international dimension may trigger additional reporting obligations, such as the above-mentioned Foreign Account Tax Compliance Act (FATCA) or Common

Reporting Standards (CRS) requirements. Tax professionals can help navigate these complex reporting obligations to avoid penalties and legal consequences.

Professional advice emphasizes the importance of maintaining comprehensive documentation and accurate records of cryptocurrency transactions. Proper record-keeping enables individuals to substantiate their tax positions, deductions, and compliance with reporting requirements. Furthermore, tax professionals can provide guidance on the timing of cryptocurrency transactions to optimize tax outcomes. They analyze holding periods to determine short-term or long-term capital gains tax rates, taking into account the individual's tax bracket and specific regulations.

For businesses engaged in cryptocurrency activities, tax professionals can assist in selecting suitable legal structures and entities to optimize tax positions. They can advise on the implications of partnerships, corporations, or limited liability companies (LLCs) and develop tax-efficient strategies.

Tax professionals specializing in international taxation can help navigate the complexities of cross-border cryptocurrency transactions. They provide insights into tax treaties, foreign tax credits, and the implications of doing business in multiple jurisdictions. They can also assist individuals in understanding and managing the legal risks associated with cryptocurrency taxation. They ensure compliance with regulatory requirements, minimize exposure to penalties, and mitigate the risk of audits or investigations.

Tax attorneys or certified public accountants may issue guidance or interpretations specific to cryptocurrencies. They can also provide interpretations and insights into these guidelines, helping individuals understand and apply them correctly. Furthermore, they can help individuals anticipate potential changes in tax laws and develop strategies to adapt to future regulatory requirements.

Conclusion

Given the complexities and evolving nature of cryptocurrency taxation, seeking professional advice for tax planning and compliance is crucial. Tax professionals equipped with the specialized knowledge and experience in cryptocurrency taxation can provide valuable insights, ensuring accurate reporting, optimizing tax positions, and mitigating legal risks. By partnering with tax experts, individuals and businesses can navigate the intricate tax landscape surrounding cryptocurrencies, foster compliance, and make informed financial decisions within the legal framework. Embracing professional advice is a proactive step towards managing tax obligations effectively and maximizing the benefits of participating in the cryptocurrency ecosystem.

Chapter Nine

Managing Risk and Avoiding Scams

The rapidly evolving world of cryptocurrencies presents a range of opportunities for investors and users. However, it also provides an opening for enterprising charlatans and scammers. As the popularity of cryptocurrencies continues to grow, it is crucial for individuals to adopt effective risk management strategies and be vigilant to avoid falling victim to swindles.

Identifying Common Cryptocurrency Scams and Frauds Targeting Seniors

As the popularity of cryptocurrencies continues to grow, it is crucial for individuals to mitigate risk and be vigilant to avoid being cleaned out by clever con-men. According to a recent Reuters article by Tad Simons, entitled *Crypto Scams Targeting Seniors Are On the Rise*, we read, "According to the FBI's 2021 Elder Fraud Report, seniors over 60 lost more than $1.7 billion to fraud last year (a 74% increase from 2020), with the average victim losing $18,246. In fact, people over 60 lost $239 million in 2021 to investment schemes alone, many of which were get-rich-quick scams involving digital assets, or cryptocurrencies. And it is estimated that for every 1 complaint the FBI receives, 44 go unreported."

Generally speaking, cryptocurrencies operate within

a digital ecosystem, making them susceptible to cybersecurity threats. Hacking attempts, phishing attacks, and theft of private keys can result in the loss of funds. Implementing robust security measures is crucial.

Unlike legacy financial systems, cryptocurrencies often operate outside the realm of traditional regulatory frameworks. This absence of investor protection measures, such as deposit insurance or recourse mechanisms, can expose individuals to greater risks. Thoroughly understanding the basics of cryptocurrencies, underlying technologies, and market dynamics is essential. Conduct extensive research, stay updated with news and industry developments, and seek reliable sources of information.

Before investing in a cryptocurrency project, conduct comprehensive due diligence. Evaluate the project's team, technology, prospectus, and reputation. Scrutinize the credibility and transparency of the project before committing funds.

Implement strong security measures to protect cryptocurrency holdings. Utilize hardware wallets or cold storage solutions that store private keys offline. Implement multi-factor authentication, strong passwords, and regularly update security software to safeguard against cyber threats.

Be conscious of phishing scam techniques. Exercise caution when receiving unsolicited messages or emails requesting personal information or cryptocurrency details. Avoid clicking on suspicious links or providing sensitive information to unverified sources.

Use reputable cryptocurrency exchanges and wallets. Research the exchange's history, security practices, and user reviews before opening an account. Ensure that exchanges have proper licensing and comply with relevant regulations.

Be wary of investment opportunities promising exceptionally high returns with little risk. Use critical thinking and avoid falling for "get-rich-quick" schemes or Ponzi schemes that rely on new investors' funds to pay existing participants.

Consult with legal and financial professionals who specialize in cryptocurrencies. They can provide insights into local regulations, investment strategies, and help identify potential red flags or scams.

If you encounter a cryptocurrency-related scam or fraud, report it to the appropriate authorities in your jurisdiction. File a complaint with local law enforcement, consumer protection agencies, or financial regulatory bodies to help prevent others from falling victim to similar scams. Contribute to raising awareness about cryptocurrency fraud. Share information about common scams, warning signs, and best practices with friends, family, and online communities to help protect others from falling prey to fraudulent schemes.

Managing risks and avoiding scams is crucial in the world of cryptocurrencies. By understanding the risks associated with cryptocurrencies, adopting effective risk management strategies, and staying vigilant against scams, individuals can protect their investments and participate safely in the cryptocurrency ecosystem. Education, due diligence, secure storage practices, and seeking professional advice are paramount to mitigating risks and ensuring a secure and rewarding cryptocurrency experience. By prioritizing safety and remaining vigilant, individuals can navigate the cryptocurrency landscape with confidence and safeguard their financial well-being.

Implementing Strategies to Protect Against Identity Theft and Financial Losses

Cryptocurrency rackets have become increasingly prevalent, targeting individuals from all walks of life. Unfortunately, senior citizens are particularly vulnerable to these schemes due to factors such as limited technology literacy, financial vulnerabilities, and a trusting nature. Exacerbating this situation is that, as the OECD countries get older demographically, senior citizens account for the wealthiest age-cohort. (In the United States, for example, people over the age of 70 control 75% of the wealth in America.) Such individuals present a tempting target to unscrupulous fraudsters.

But there are ways to protect yourself. Be conscious of the traps.

Ponzi and pyramid schemes are among the oldest and most common scams in the financial world. They involve promising high returns to investors, primarily relying on funds from new investors to pay previous investors.

Be vigilant regarding obvious red flags. Promises of exceptionally high and guaranteed returns with little to no risk are unrealistic and often indicative of fraudulent schemes. Schemes that prioritize recruitment of new investors rather than the actual value or use of the cryptocurrency should raise suspicions. Scammers may provide limited information about the investment, its underlying technology, or the team behind the project. Fraudsters may also employ aggressive tactics to convince seniors to invest quickly, creating a sense of urgency or fear of missing out (FOMO).

Phishing scams (which we addressed earlier) involve fraudsters impersonating legitimate entities, such as cryptocurrency exchanges or wallet providers, in order to trick individuals into revealing sensitive information or transferring funds.

In addition, be wary of unsolicited emails, text messages, or phone calls requesting personal information or cryptocurrency details. Likewise, avoid clicking on links provided in unsolicited messages, as they may lead to fake websites designed to steal login credentials or install malware.

Many phishing messages contain grammatical errors or spelling mistakes, which can be a sign of an illegitimate communication. According to the con artists themselves, these unprofessional typographical errors are no accident. They're used to weed out what they see as intelligent people, exposing the gullible upon whom they're planning to prey.

CRYPTOCURRENCY FOR SENIORS

Fake Initial Coin Offerings (ICOs) are also a problem. These involve scammers creating fraudulent cryptocurrency projects and soliciting investments from unsuspecting individuals. These initiatives often promise innovative technology or significant returns but fail to deliver.

Scammers may present vague or unrealistic project ideas without a clear roadmap or evidence of technical capabilities. Fake ICOs often provide minimal or fabricated information about the team members, their expertise, or their involvement in the project.

Another common con are impersonation scams. These involve fraudsters posing as well-known individuals or cryptocurrency influencers to deceive individuals into sending them money or cryptocurrencies. Beware of messages from strangers claiming to be influential figures or offering investment opportunities. Cross-check the identity of individuals claiming to be public figures by verifying their social media accounts or official websites. Legitimate individuals or organizations will never ask for private keys or sensitive account information.

Tips to Protect Against Scams and Frauds:

1. Educate Yourself: Stay informed about the latest scams and fraud techniques targeting seniors. Attend workshops or seminars focused on cryptocurrency safety and fraud prevention.

2. Verify Sources: Always verify the legitimacy of cryptocurrency exchanges, projects, or

investment opportunities by conducting thorough research, checking official websites, and reading user reviews.

3. Exercise Caution Online: Be cautious when sharing personal information online or engaging in financial transactions. Avoid clicking on suspicious links and be skeptical of unsolicited messages or calls.

4. Seek Professional Advice: Consult with trusted financial advisors or legal professionals who specialize in cryptocurrency to ensure you make informed decisions and avoid potential scams.

Cryptocurrency scams and frauds targeting seniors can have devastating financial consequences. By understanding common scam tactics, recognizing red flags, and adopting preventive measures, seniors can protect themselves from falling victim to fraudulent schemes. Ongoing education, vigilance, and seeking professional advice are crucial to navigating the cryptocurrency landscape safely. It is essential for seniors to stay informed, trust their instincts, and verify the legitimacy of cryptocurrency investments or opportunities before making any financial decisions. By equipping themselves with knowledge and awareness, seniors can safeguard their investments and enjoy the benefits of cryptocurrencies while avoiding the pitfalls of scams and fraud.

CRYPTOCURRENCY FOR SENIORS

Recognizing Red Flags and Conducting Due Diligence Before Investing

According to the Federal Bureau of Investigation in the United States, crypto scams surged a staggering 78%, year-over-year, in 2022. In America alone, senior citizens were robbed of over a billion dollars. It was a four-fold increase over the past twelve months.

Seniors are often tricked by charlatans claiming to "let them in" on clever schemes to manipulate cryptocurrency fluctuations in order to make a profit, or enticing them with claims of participating in a lottery, or other alluring (though phony) business plans.

Carefully read the project's whitepaper, which outlines the concept, technology, and goals. Assess the viability and legitimacy of the project based on its proposed use-case and innovation.

Investigate the backgrounds and experience of the project team members. Look for evidence of their expertise, previous successful projects, or relevant industry experience.

Evaluate the level of community engagement surrounding the project. Active and supportive communities can indicate a higher level of credibility and legitimacy.

Assess the technological aspects of the cryptocurrency, including its underlying blockchain technology and consensus mechanism. Assess whether the technology offers unique advantages or innovations compared to existing solutions.

Consider partnerships or collaborations the project has established with reputable organizations or industry leaders. These can demonstrate the project's credibility and potential for wider adoption.

Research the regulatory landscape of the cryptocurrency in the relevant jurisdiction. Check if the project complies with applicable laws and regulations.

Determine if the cryptocurrency project or platform holds necessary licenses or registrations. Look for evidence of compliance with financial and securities regulations.

In addition, seek opinions from independent experts, cryptocurrency influencers, or reputable media outlets. Analyze their assessments of the project's potential, risks, and long-term viability.

Engage with the cryptocurrency community through forums, social media platforms, or dedicated cryptocurrency communities. Seek insights from experienced investors and learn from their experiences.

In compliance with all the rules of risk management, set a clear investment strategy and define risk tolerance levels. Diversify your cryptocurrency investments across different projects and asset classes to minimize exposure to any single investment.

Implement robust security measures to protect your cryptocurrency investments. Consider consulting with financial advisors or cryptocurrency experts who can provide personalized guidance tailored to your investment goals and risk appetite.

Conclusion

Investing in cryptocurrencies can be rewarding, but it requires caution and due diligence. Recognizing red flags and conducting thorough research are essential steps to mitigate risks and make informed investment decisions. By understanding the market, recognizing warning signs, conducting due diligence on cryptocurrency projects, and seeking professional advice when necessary, individuals can protect themselves from rackets and fraudulent schemes. Remember that knowledge and research are key to successful cryptocurrency investing. Be vigilant, stay informed, and approach investments with a balanced perspective to maximize the potential rewards while minimizing the associated risks.

Chapter Ten

The Future of Cryptocurrency

Cryptocurrency has emerged as a groundbreaking technology with the potential to revolutionize the financial landscape. According to a recent article by Joshua Ramos, "BlackRock CEO Larry Fink says crypto will transcend international currencies due to its worldwide demand. Moreover, Fink described crypto as an 'international asset' that has a 'differentiating value versus other asset classes' while speaking of the opportunity and interest in the crypto sector."

This section explores the potential directions and developments that could shape the future of cryptocurrency and its impact on various aspects of our lives.

Discussing Emerging Trends and Implications of the Technology, Geopolitically

The world of cryptocurrency continues to evolve at a rapid pace, driven by technological advancements and innovative ideas. As the popularity of cryptocurrencies grows, so do questions about where this will lead. The allure of cryptocurrencies are that they allow for more decentralized transactions. However, there are those who fear that, ultimately (over the long run), the technology may be used to centralize power.

For instance, in the admission that cryptos may be a cause for annoyance when dealing with different jurisdictions, subtle pushes may be made to "harmonize international laws" in terms of taxation and reporting. If this is achieved, then it may become a truly "global currency".

Political integration usually follows economic integration. As Mayer Anselm Rothschild said in 1790, "Permit me to issue and control the money of a nation, and I care not who makes its laws."

In other words, the laws will "follow the money".

90% of a government's power comes from its control of the currency. If it loses this, its influence will ebb away to a remarkable (though predictable) degree. So, with cryptocurrency possibly becoming a "global unit of exchange," regional nation-states will lose much of their relevance as the outlines for a planetary super-state emerge.

The creation of the European Union might offer itself as an example for this happening on a smaller, regional scale. The political confederation began as an economic integration pact in 1957 with the Treaty of Rome. This trade agreement created the so-called European Economic Community (EEC).

Ever since its introduction, there were deepening integration efforts. Over time, the EEC expanded its scope beyond economic matters. Member states were told they needed closer cooperation in areas such as agriculture, regional development, border policy and common issues of concern like competition and trade. These efforts aimed to deepen integration and address common challenges.

Soon afterward they created supranational institutions to manage the growing complexity of economic integration. Some of these new institutions were the European Commission, the European Parliament, and the Court of Justice. These institutions helped create a framework for concentrated power, fostering a centralized governance structure .

January 1, 1999 saw the introduction of a common currency, the Euro. This further tied the individual nation-states together as subordinate units in one larger "federalized" super-state. Once-sovereign countries within the EU lost much of their power and autonomy.

Over a long enough time-horizon, it is not unforeseeable that a similar phenomenon might occur globally, as cryptocurrencies tie the international community together and foster greater cooperation.

As with all innovations, there is usually a diversity of options at the dawn of the tech. Over time, however, these choices whittle away down to one or two. For instance, when auto manufacturing began in the United States there were hundreds of corporations producing cars. Over the course of a century, however, this contracted to three or four large manufactures in the sector. According to Tim Wu, in his book, *The Master Switch*, this is the norm for any new technology.

CoinMarketCap, as of the writing of this book, said that there are 22,932 different cryptocurrencies in the world. Don't expect that to be the case in fifty years.

Or even twenty.

If cryptocurrencies conform to the standard trend, then the inefficient versions of the technology will wither and be supplanted by a few winners.

Currently Central Banks are trying to roll out their own version of cryprocurrency, named Central Bank Digital Currency (CBDC).

Central Bank Digital Currency

As the U.S. dollar's future as the world reserve currency comes into doubt, there are several challenges to its dominance. A rival bloc of nations, known colloquially as the BRICS countries (which stands for Brazil, Russia, India, China and South Africa) seem bent on creating their own parallel economic system that is no longer dependent on the dollar. They are currently planning on introducing their own rival currency (which will have precious metal-backing). What's interesting is that this currency will defy the historical norm of money being tied to a particular country and will be used by a whole range of nations.

Likewise Brazil and Argentina are currently in talks about creating a joint currency that will cross borders.

The future seems to suggest that individual national currencies will yield to regional or continental currencies, before, at length, being supplanted by one global currency.

But in the short term, central bank digital currencies are emerging as a sort of transitional stage.

Their proponents promise greater efficiency and accessibility with respect to the CBDCs. They are said to enable instant and cost-effective peer-to-peer transactions, providing financial services to the unbanked and underbanked populations. It promotes financial inclusion by allowing individuals without traditional bank accounts to access digital payment systems securely.

CBDCs have the potential to simplify cross-border transactions, reducing intermediaries, transaction costs, and processing times. This can significantly enhance global trade, remittance flows, and economic integration.

CBDCs offer central banks a direct channel to implement monetary policy, enabling more effective and precise control over interest rates, money supply, and inflation. This direct influence on the economy can support stability and facilitate economic growth.

They are said to be able to enhance financial stability by providing regulators with real-time visibility into transactions, enabling proactive monitoring and mitigation of risks such as money laundering, fraud, and illicit activities.

This greater control over people's private transactions and ability to remotely monitor the economic habits of citizens has some civil libertarians sounding an alarm. Especially after the government in Canada imposed punitive action against citizens who engaged in a political protest at the Trucker's Rally in 2022.

The government, in many cases, punished dissidents by "unbanking them" and effectively shutting off their money.

CBDCs have this inherent capability.

Central banks will also be able to encourage people to spend money (thus "goosing" the economy) by having "expiration dates" on currency, like China's CDBC (the Digital Yuan) does. Whatever you don't spend at the end of the month disappears. This will, of course, prevent wealth aggregation and discourage the concept of saving.

Exploring the Potential Impact of Cryptocurrencies on Global Finance

Cryptocurrencies have emerged as a disruptive force in the financial landscape, challenging traditional systems and offering new possibilities for global finance and political structures. This section drills down on the potential impact of cryptocurrencies on global finance, examining how they can revolutionize areas such as cross-border transactions, financial inclusion, monetary policy, and the role of central banks. By exploring these potential effects, we can gain insights into the transformative power of cryptocurrencies and their implications for the future of global finance.

Cryptocurrencies will likely foster increased "globalism" by enabling faster and more cost-effective cross-border transactions by eliminating intermediaries and reducing transaction fees. This can significantly benefit individuals and businesses, especially in regions where traditional banking infrastructure is limited.

CRYPTOCURRENCY FOR SENIORS

Cryptocurrencies have the potential to provide financial services to the unbanked and underbanked populations globally. By offering accessible and inclusive financial solutions, cryptocurrencies can empower individuals and facilitate economic growth in underserved areas.

Cryptocurrencies bypass the need for traditional intermediaries such as banks, allowing individuals to engage in direct peer-to-peer transactions. This disintermediation can reduce costs, increase transparency, and provide greater control over personal finances.

With cryptocurrencies, individuals can become their own bank, managing their funds and assets independently. This decentralization of financial power shifts control from centralized authorities to individuals, enhancing financial sovereignty and autonomy.

In other words, the future will not be a Central Bank, a commercial bank and then you. It will cut out the middle man, with CBDCs creating a new model of the Central Bank and you. The commercial banks you knew and grew up with will become largely obsolete. As will many industries associated with the old system . . . like accountants, payment processors, money transfer services (like Western Union or MoneyGram), regulatory and compliance professionals, currency exchanges, and so forth.

Conclusion

It's important to note that while some careers may face disruption, the emergence of cryptocurrencies and blockchain technology also presents new opportunities. New roles related to blockchain development, smart contract programming, cybersecurity, and digital asset management are already in demand and likely to grow in the future. As with any technological shift, it is crucial for individuals in affected fields to adapt their skills and knowledge to remain relevant in the evolving job market.

significant. Older individuals may allocate their resources towards assisting their children or grandchildren with education, housing, or other financial needs. This may impact their purchasing habits, shifting focus from personal consumption to supporting younger generations.

According to the World Health Organization, "By 2030, 1 in 6 people in the world will be aged 60 years or over. At this time the share of the population aged 60 years and over will increase from 1 billion in 2020 to 1.4 billion. By 2050, the world's population of people aged 60 years and older will double (2.1 billion)."

Seniors tend to have different priorities in life . . . such as creating bucket lists that focus more on travel, for instance. They like to explore new places, both domestic and international, and tick off destinations from their travel wishlist. This may include iconic landmarks, natural wonders, cultural sites, or places of personal significance.

Before we move on to other bucket list items, let's start with how cryptos can help facilitate travel.

Cryptocurrency and Travel

Cryptocurrencies can offer several benefits for those engaging in tourism and excursions. Since they're decentralized and operate on a global scale, cryptocurrencies allow for seamless and borderless transactions. This can simplify cross-border payments, eliminating the need for currency exchange and reducing transaction fees and delays associated with traditional banking systems. Travelers can make direct peer-to-peer cryptocurrency payments, making international transactions more efficient.

Likewise, cryptocurrencies can reduce transaction costs, particularly for international travelers. Traditional payment methods, such as credit cards or wire transfers, often involve various fees, including foreign transaction fees, currency conversion fees, and bank charges. Cryptocurrencies can mitigate or eliminate many of these fees, enabling travelers to save money on transactions.

Moreover, this new method will enable transactions to be processed quickly, especially when compared to traditional banking systems that may involve intermediaries and multiple clearance stages. This speed can be advantageous for travelers, allowing them to make immediate payments for bookings, accommodations, or services, even in time-sensitive situations.

Furthermore, cryptocurrencies provide a high level of security through advanced cryptographic techniques. Travelers can use them for transactions without sharing sensitive financial information, reducing the risk of identity theft or fraud. Additionally, blockchain technology, which underlies cryptocurrencies, offers transparency and immutability, enhancing trust and security in travel-related transactions.

Six travel sites that accept cryptocurrencies are:

1. Bitcoin.Travel
2. Travala.com
3. Cheapair.com
4. Alternative Airlines
5. Destinia.com
6. Travelbybit.com

In addition, there are many national parks and historical sites that now accept cryptocurrencies. As well as other tourism destinations, such as . . . for example:

1. Switzerland: Switzerland, known for its progressive approach to cryptocurrencies, has several tourism destinations that accept cryptocurrencies. For instance, the town of Zug, also known as "Crypto Valley," has accepted Bitcoin as a form of payment for public services since 2016. Additionally, some hotels, restaurants, and tourism companies in Switzerland, particularly in major cities like Zurich and Geneva, may accept cryptocurrencies.

2. Japan: Japan has been at the forefront of cryptocurrency adoption, recognizing Bitcoin as legal tender since 2017. Some businesses in Japan's major cities, such as Tokyo, have started accepting cryptocurrencies, including hotels, restaurants, and travel agencies.

3. Bali, Indonesia: Bali, a popular tourist destination in Indonesia, has witnessed increasing acceptance of cryptocurrencies.

Some businesses, including hotels, resorts, and restaurants, have begun accepting cryptocurrencies like Bitcoin as a payment option.

4. Prague, Czech Republic: Prague, the capital city of the Czech Republic, has a reputation for being cryptocurrency-friendly. Several hotels, restaurants, and even souvenir shops in Prague accept cryptocurrencies.

5. Overstock.com: While not a specific tourism destination, Overstock.com is an online retailer that accepts various cryptocurrencies for purchasing travel-related products, including flights, hotels, and car rentals.

Reconnecting with family and friends becomes evermore important as people age. Building and strengthening relationships with loved ones takes center stage as a person's true priorities come to the fore. Managing your finances more efficiently can open up new possibilities in organizing family reunions, visiting grandchildren, or reconnecting with old friends.

Cryptocurrency and Hobbies

Pursuing hobbies and interests are important as seniors approach their golden years. Engaging in activities they are passionate about, such as painting, gardening, playing musical instruments, writing, or cooking is important for seniors.

Some of the varied things that might be pursued are:

1. Art and Collectibles: Cryptocurrencies have gained popularity in the world of digital art and collectibles. Platforms like NFT (Non-Fungible Token) marketplaces allow artists and collectors to buy and sell digital artwork or unique digital assets using cryptocurrencies.

2. Sports and Fitness: Fitness trainers, sports coaches, and gyms may accept cryptocurrencies as a form of payment for their services. Additionally, sports equipment and apparel stores may offer the option to purchase items using cryptocurrencies.

3. Online Courses and Education: Various online learning platforms and educational institutions accept cryptocurrencies as payment for courses, certifications, and educational materials. This allows individuals to expand their knowledge and skills using digital currencies.

4. Music and Streaming Services: Independent musicians and content creators often accept cryptocurrencies for their music albums, merchandise, or access to exclusive content. Some streaming platforms and online music stores also offer the option to purchase music or subscribe to services using cryptocurrencies.

5. Gadgets and Electronics: Some online retailers that sell gadgets, electronics, or tech-related products accept cryptocurrencies as a

payment option. This can include purchases of smartphones, computers, gaming consoles, and other tech gadgets.

6. Charitable Donations: Cryptocurrencies can be donated to charitable organizations and causes. Many nonprofits and charities have started accepting cryptocurrencies as a means of supporting their initiatives.

And speaking of charitable donations, a big change in economic behavior as someone gets older is an emerging interest in volunteer work and philanthropy.

Cryptocurrency and Philanthropy

Giving back to the community and making a positive impact through volunteer work, supporting charitable causes, or mentoring younger generations is a healthy preoccupation for seniors.

In recent years, the advent of cryptocurrencies and the rise of crowdsourcing platforms have revolutionized the way individuals can support and uplift others in need. GoFundMe, KickStarter, Indiegogo, Fundition, and similar crowdsourcing websites have embraced cryptocurrencies as a means to extend the reach and impact of philanthropy. Individuals can now help make a difference on a global scale.

Cryptocurrencies (as alluded to before) facilitate borderless transactions, allowing individuals to donate to causes and organizations globally without the need for traditional banking systems. This is particularly beneficial for supporting causes in countries with limited access to financial services or in disaster-stricken regions where immediate assistance is crucial.

Cryptocurrencies can significantly reduce transaction costs associated with traditional payment methods. By eliminating intermediaries and streamlining the donation process, more of the donated amount reaches the intended beneficiaries, maximizing the impact of philanthropic efforts.

Blockchain technology provides transparency and immutability. Donors can track the flow of funds on the blockchain, ensuring transparency in charitable transactions. This transparency helps build trust and confidence in philanthropic organizations, promoting accountability and reducing the risk of corruption.

In addition, cryptocurrencies allow for micropayments, enabling individuals to donate even very small amounts of cryptocurrency. This can foster a culture of fractional giving, where individuals collectively make a significant impact through cumulative small donations.

Moreover, cryptocurrencies offer the option of anonymous donations, allowing donors to protect their privacy. While transparency is beneficial in many cases, some donors prefer to remain anonymous, and cryptocurrencies provide an avenue to do so.

Cryptocurrency and Personal Development

Learning and personal development acquire a new allure for seniors as they transition to a new stage of their life. Many want to continue to expand their knowledge and skills through lifelong learning, whether it's pursuing a degree, taking up new courses, attending workshops, or learning a new language.

Blockchain technology has enabled the emergence of decentralized learning platforms and educational ecosystems. These platforms leverage cryptocurrencies and blockchain to offer educational resources, certifications, or mentoring services. Senior citizens can leverage these platforms to explore new areas of interest, acquire new skills, or engage in lifelong learning.

Furthermore, cryptocurrencies can facilitate peer-to-peer learning and mentorship opportunities. Senior citizens can connect with mentors or experts in various fields through decentralized platforms, utilizing cryptocurrencies as a means of compensation for their guidance or expertise. This fosters a collaborative learning environment and promotes intergenerational knowledge exchange.

Cryptocurrencies and blockchain technology can enable the tokenization of credentials and certifications. Senior citizens can leverage these digital credentials to showcase their expertise or complete courses, making it easier to validate their skills and knowledge in various domains.

Many institutions of higher education accept cryptocurrency as a form of payment, such as:

1. Lucerne University of Applied Sciences and Arts (Switzerland): Lucerne University of Applied Sciences and Arts announced in 2020 that it would accept Bitcoin as a payment method for tuition fees.

2. European University Cyprus (Cyprus): European University Cyprus has reportedly been accepting Bitcoin as a payment option for tuition fees since 2013, making it one of the early adopters in the education sector.

3. King's College (New York, USA): King's College, a liberal arts college located in New York, began accepting Bitcoin as a payment option for tuition in 2014.

4. Cumbria University (United Kingdom): Cumbria University, based in the United Kingdom, announced in 2018 that it would accept Bitcoin as a form of payment for two of its courses related to cryptocurrencies and blockchain.

5. The University of British Columbia (Canada): The University of British Columbia's Blockchain@UBC initiative has explored the integration of cryptocurrencies and blockchain technology. While it may not accept cryptocurrencies for tuition fees, the university has engaged in research and educational activities in the field.

Not only can you take classes or expand your human capital, but you can use cryptocurrencies to help your grandchildren achieve *their* academic goals, as well.

Cryptocurrency and Health

Cryptocurrencies have the potential to transform the way senior citizens maintain an active and healthy lifestyle, offering new opportunities for engagement, access to services, and financial empowerment. Cryptocurrencies can serve as incentives for senior citizens to adopt and maintain an active lifestyle. By participating in fitness programs or wellness initiatives that reward physical activity with cryptocurrencies, seniors can receive tangible benefits for engaging in exercise. This incentive-based system not only promotes regular physical activity but also instills a sense of achievement and motivation among senior citizens.

Cryptocurrencies enable senior citizens to access a wide range of online health and wellness services. Through telehealth platforms and decentralized health applications, seniors can consult doctors, therapists, and fitness experts remotely, without the need for extensive travel or physical visits. Cryptocurrencies facilitate secure and efficient payment for these services, enhancing access to personalized healthcare solutions and expert guidance.

Cryptocurrencies can encourage seniors to explore the world of digital currencies and engage in mental stimulation. By participating in blockchain-based games, quizzes, or educational platforms, seniors can exercise their cognitive abilities while learning about new monetary innovations. This mental stimulation can contribute to improved memory, attention, and overall cognitive health among senior citizens.

Cryptocurrencies can facilitate community engagement and social connections for senior citizens. Through blockchain-based social platforms or decentralized applications, seniors can connect with like-minded individuals, join interest groups, or participate in philanthropic initiatives. These platforms provide opportunities for networking, sharing experiences, and building meaningful relationships, combating social isolation and enhancing overall well-being.

Cryptocurrencies have the potential to empower senior citizens to embrace nature and outdoor activities, providing new avenues for exploration, adventure, and wellness. Platforms utilizing blockchain technology can offer opportunities for seniors to book nature retreats, outdoor excursions, or eco-tours, making it convenient to explore different natural landscapes and engage in thrilling experiences.

By accepting cryptocurrencies, nature tour operators, parks, and outdoor activity providers can streamline payment processes, eliminating the need for physical cash or traditional banking systems. This convenience enhances the overall experience for seniors, allowing them to focus on enjoying their outdoor adventures.

Through blockchain-based rewards programs, seniors

can earn digital tokens for engaging in outdoor exercises, hiking, or participating in nature conservation initiatives. Through the same platform or online communities, seniors can share their outdoor experiences, exchange tips and recommendations, and plan group excursions. These connections foster a sense of belonging and create a supportive network of individuals passionate about nature and outdoor activities.

Cryptocurrencies and Exploring Cultural Experiences

Seniors can attend concerts, theater performances, art exhibitions, or museums to immerse themselves in various forms of art and cultural expressions. By embracing digital currencies, senior citizens can unlock a world of heritage sites, cultural events, and immersive encounters that transcend physical boundaries.

Cryptocurrencies enable senior citizens to access global cultural platforms, such as virtual museums, art galleries, and digital archives. Through blockchain technology, these platforms can offer exclusive exhibitions, historical artifacts, and interactive experiences that bring culture and heritage to life. Senior citizens can use cryptocurrencies to gain entry to these digital realms and explore diverse cultural treasures from the comfort of their homes.

Senior citizens can use cryptocurrencies to support local artists and artisans around the world. By purchasing artwork, handicrafts, or cultural products with cryptocurrencies, seniors contribute directly to the preservation and promotion of traditional crafts and artistic endeavors. This form of patronage encourages cultural sustainability and fosters a deeper appreciation for the diverse artistic expressions found in different regions.

Cryptocurrencies enable the tokenization of cultural experiences. By participating in tokenized events or cultural projects, senior citizens can acquire digital tokens that represent their engagement and support. These tokens can provide access to exclusive cultural events, guided tours, or behind-the-scenes experiences that deepen their understanding and connection with local cultures.

Through cryptocurrency-based crowdfunding campaigns, seniors can contribute to the preservation of historical sites, language revitalization programs, or community-driven cultural events. By supporting these initiatives, seniors actively contribute to cultural preservation and encourage sustainable practices.

Cryptocurrencies facilitate cultural exchange and collaboration among senior citizens worldwide. Blockchain-based social platforms enable seniors to connect with individuals from diverse cultural backgrounds, fostering dialogue, sharing experiences, and creating meaningful connections. These platforms provide opportunities for seniors to engage in intercultural discussions, exchange stories and traditions, and participate in virtual cultural exchange programs.

In short, cryptocurrencies have opened doors for

senior citizens to embark on exciting cultural journeys, expanding their horizons and fostering a deep appreciation for global cultural diversity. Through cryptocurrencies, seniors can access virtual cultural platforms, support local artists, engage in cultural tourism, and participate in tokenized cultural experiences. By leveraging blockchain technology, senior citizens can connect with like-minded individuals, support cultural initiatives, and engage in meaningful cultural exchange. Cryptocurrencies empower senior citizens to explore cultural experiences, bridging gaps, and enriching their lives through the wonders of global cultural heritage.

Cryptocurrencies and Family History

Cryptocurrencies offer senior citizens a transformative means to document their life stories, memories, and family history, ensuring that their legacy is preserved for future generations. Senior citizens can utilize various mediums, such as writing, photography, or audiovisual recordings, to share their experiences in a secure and accessible manner. They now have the means to protect and digitize their personal archives. By leveraging blockchain technology, seniors can store their written accounts, photographs, letters, or other personal artifacts in a decentralized and tamper-proof manner. This ensures that their legacy remains intact, protected from loss, damage, or deterioration.

Cryptocurrencies enable senior citizens to fund creative projects focused on documenting their genealogy and family history. Through crowdfunding platforms and cryptocurrency donations, seniors can seek support for writing books, producing documentaries, or creating multimedia projects that encapsulate their experiences. These funds help ensure the realization and preservation of their artistic endeavors for future generations.

Senior citizens can leverage cryptocurrencies to tokenize memorabilia associated with their life stories or family history. Non-fungible tokens (NFTs) can represent items like handwritten letters, heirlooms, or significant objects. By minting NFTs, seniors establish a verifiable and unique digital representation of their personal artifacts, preserving their sentimental value and allowing future generations to experience their legacy.

Cryptocurrencies encourage collaborative storytelling platforms where senior citizens can engage with family members, friends, or fellow seniors to collectively document their life stories and family history. Through blockchain-enabled platforms, individuals can contribute their own narratives, photographs, or anecdotes, creating a rich tapestry of memories that capture the essence of their shared experiences.

Cryptocurrencies and Accomplishing Personal Goals

Using the Blockchain technology associated with cryptocurrencies is not just about recording and preserving the past, but about making *new* memories.

CRYPTOCURRENCY FOR SENIORS

Older citizens can set and achieve personal goals, such as embarking on an adventurous activity like skydiving or hot air ballooning. Or creating quality time with grandchildren.

By embracing digital currencies, elderly people can explore new avenues for planning vacations, organizing family outings, and celebrating special events. This can facilitate the creation of unforgettable moments and strengthen familial bonds among seniors and their loved ones.

Cryptocurrencies provide senior citizens with opportunities for collaborative travel planning. Through decentralized travel platforms or smart contract-based arrangements, seniors can engage with family members in decision-making processes, collectively choosing destinations, accommodations, and activities. Cryptocurrencies allow for transparent budgeting and expense tracking, ensuring a shared sense of involvement and investment in the planning process.

Multi-generational learning opportunities for senior citizens and their families can be had via the infrastructure that underlies cryptocurrency. By engaging in educational platforms or blockchain-based projects, seniors can share their knowledge and experiences with younger family members. This intergenerational exchange cultivates mutual understanding and fosters discussions about financial literacy, technology, and the evolving landscape of digital currencies.

And speaking of young ones . . .

CRYPTOCURRENCY FOR SENIORS

Cryptocurrencies give senior citizens a powerful tool to support and encourage their grandchildren's passions and talents. They can provide financial resources for extracurricular activities, lessons, or equipment, enabling their grandchildren to explore and develop their interests. They can fund a wide range of activities that align with their grandchildren's interests. Whether it's music lessons, art classes, sports programs, or coding workshops, cryptocurrencies offer a flexible payment option for enrollment fees, equipment purchases, or participation expenses.

Whether it's musical instruments, art supplies, sports gear, or technological devices, senior citizens can use cryptocurrencies to help provide the resources needed for their grandchildren's pursuits.

A side benefit of using the new technology is that it also fosters their grandkids' economic literacy and encourages entrepreneurialism. Through crowdfunding platforms utilizing cryptocurrencies, grandchildren can receive financial backing for their startups, inventions, or creative initiatives.

By providing resources for extracurricular activities, lessons, or equipment, senior citizens show their belief in their grandchildren's talents and passions. This support fosters self-confidence, determination, and a sense of purpose, helping grandchildren develop important life skills and shaping their character positively.

Conclusion

Cryptocurrencies offer senior citizens an innovative means to pursue their goals and fulfill their bucket list aspirations. By embracing digital currencies, seniors can overcome financial barriers, access unique opportunities, and make their dreams a reality. Blockchain technology also enables seniors to share their experiences, create legacies, and inspire others. By embracing digital currencies, seniors embark on transformative journeys of self-discovery, personal growth, and the strengthening of familial bonds.

Chapter Twelve
Planning for the Future

Cryptocurrencies have emerged as a crucial consideration for senior citizens when planning for the future, particularly regarding their end-of-life arrangements and estate management. As digital assets, cryptocurrencies require specific attention to ensure their secure transfer and distribution to beneficiaries. This section explores the importance of cryptocurrency for senior citizens in end-of-life planning, estate management, and preserving their digital legacies.

Cryptocurrency and Estate Planning

Cryptocurrencies have emerged as a vital component in estate planning, ensuring that family members are taken care of in the long term. By integrating digital currencies into estate planning strategies, individuals can safeguard their assets and provide clear instructions for the management and distribution of their wealth. Here we will unpack information about estate planning, including wills, trusts, and healthcare directives to secure the financial well-being of loved ones.

First off, without appropriate measures, the loss or mismanagement of assets can lead to substantial financial setbacks for family members. Including cryptocurrencies in an estate plan ensures that these digital assets are protected, properly managed, and transferred to the intended beneficiaries upon the individual's passing.

Estate planning involves drafting a comprehensive will that explicitly includes instructions for the disposition of assets. In terms of cryptocurrency, this includes designating specific digital wallets, private keys, or access information for the secure transfer of resources to chosen heirs or beneficiaries. Clearly defining beneficiary designations ensures that family members receive the intended digital assets, avoiding potential disputes or confusion.

Cryptocurrency trusts provide an effective way to manage and distribute digital assets according to the wishes of the individual. By creating a trust, individuals can designate a trustee who will oversee the administration and distribution of cryptocurrencies to beneficiaries based on predetermined conditions. Cryptocurrency trusts provide greater control, flexibility, and privacy in managing and preserving digital assets.

Mapping this all out requires careful consideration of key management and backup strategies. It is crucial to document and communicate access information, including private keys, passwords, or recovery phrases, to trusted individuals who will handle the assets in case of incapacity or death. Implementing secure storage solutions and backup protocols for these access credentials minimizes the risk of loss or unauthorized access.

Estate planning encompasses not only financial

considerations but also healthcare directives. In the event of incapacitation, individuals can include instructions for granting authorized individuals access to their cryptocurrencies to ensure ongoing management and protection of their digital assets. Healthcare directives that encompass cryptocurrency access provisions provide a comprehensive approach to estate planning for seniors.

Given the complexities of administering bequests and legacy arrangements, it is crucial to seek professional guidance from estate planning attorneys and financial advisors experienced in digital assets. These professionals can provide personalized advice, ensure compliance with legal and tax requirements, and assist in developing a comprehensive estate plan that incorporates cryptocurrencies effectively.

Estate plans should be regularly reviewed and updated to reflect changes in personal circumstances, cryptocurrency holdings, and relevant laws. As the cryptocurrency landscape evolves, it is important to stay informed about new regulations, security measures, and estate planning strategies to ensure that the estate plan remains up to date and aligned with the individual's intentions.

To recap: Cryptocurrencies have become a significant consideration in estate planning, requiring careful thought and attention to ensure the long-term security of family members. By integrating digital currencies into estate planning strategies, including wills, trusts, and healthcare directives, individuals can protect their assets, provide clear instructions for the management and distribution of cryptocurrencies, and minimize the potential for disputes or loss. Seeking professional guidance and regularly reviewing the estate plan are essential steps in ensuring that family members are well taken care of and that the benefits of cryptocurrencies are maximized in the context of estate planning.

Long-Term Care Considerations

Cryptocurrency presents senior citizens with a range of possibilities for long-term care planning, offering avenues to alleviate financial burdens for both seniors and their family members. By embracing digital currencies, seniors can explore options such as long-term care insurance, retirement communities, or in-home care, providing financial security and peace of mind.

Let's begin with long-term care insurance. These policies offer financial protection against potential healthcare costs in the future. By utilizing cryptocurrencies to pay premiums or invest in insurance products, seniors can ensure coverage for services such as assisted living, nursing care, or in-home care. Cryptocurrencies provide a secure and efficient means of managing insurance-related transactions, setting seniors' minds at ease.

In addition, cryptocurrencies offer the elderly the means to explore retirement communities or assisted living facilities that align with their needs and preferences. By utilizing digital currencies to finance entrance fees, monthly payments, or additional services, seniors can secure their place in these communities while alleviating financial burdens for themselves and their family members. Cryptocurrencies enable secure and transparent transactions, ensuring that funds are utilized for the intended purposes.

Moreover, cryptocurrencies provide senior citizens with the financial resources to access in-home care services or hire personal assistants. By utilizing digital currencies, seniors can pay for caregiving services, home modifications, or medical equipment necessary for independent living. Cryptocurrencies eliminate the need for intermediaries, reducing transaction fees and providing direct access to services that enhance seniors' quality of life.

Furthermore, cryptocurrencies facilitate the development of decentralized health insurance programs tailored to senior citizens' needs. These programs, built on blockchain technology, leverage smart contracts to provide transparent coverage, claims processing, and cost-sharing mechanisms. By participating in such programs, seniors can contribute to a community-driven insurance model that offers comprehensive and cost-effective coverage.

Cryptocurrencies enable the development of peer-to-peer care networks, connecting seniors with caregivers or other seniors who offer support services. Through blockchain-based platforms, seniors can access a wide range of services, such as companionship, transportation, or household assistance, without the need for traditional intermediaries. Cryptocurrencies provide a secure and transparent payment mechanism, ensuring fair compensation for services received.

What's more, cryptocurrencies offer senior citizens financial security and peace of mind when it comes to long-term care planning. By leveraging digital currencies, seniors can alleviate financial burdens for themselves and their family members, ensuring access to quality care and support. The transparency, security, and efficiency provided by cryptocurrencies enable seniors to navigate the complexities of long-term care planning with confidence and reassurance.

Financial Planning Together

Cryptocurrencies provide an opportunity for senior citizens to engage their families in financial planning discussions and decisions, fostering transparency and shared responsibility. By involving family members in arranging for their legacy, seniors can ensure a holistic approach to managing digital assets, understanding the technology, and preparing for the future.

First of all, cryptocurrencies offer an entry point for discussions on financial technology, fostering education and technology literacy among family members. By sharing knowledge about cryptocurrencies, blockchain technology, and digital asset management, seniors can bridge the generation gap and empower family members to understand and participate in the evolving financial landscape. This shared understanding creates a foundation for informed decision-making and collaboration.

The situation provides an opportunity for seniors to initiate transparent discussions about financial planning. Open discussions help family members understand the potential risks and enable them to provide input and support.

Family members may be drawn in for investment decisions, diversification strategies, and risk assessments. Seniors, after all, might benefit from diverse perspectives and collective wisdom. Joint decision-making promotes a sense of shared responsibility and ensures that financial planning aligns with the overall family objectives.

Cryptocurrencies can serve as a platform for inclusive financial training within the family. Seniors can facilitate learning opportunities for family members, including workshops, webinars, or discussions about investments and risk management. By fostering financial literacy and skills development, seniors empower their family members to participate actively in financial planning processes.

Cryptocurrencies introduce the need for executor and successor preparation within the family. Seniors can involve family members in the process of designating responsible individuals to manage their digital assets in the event of incapacitation or death. This involvement ensures that family members understand their roles and responsibilities regarding the transfer and management of cryptocurrencies, promoting a smooth transition and minimizing potential conflicts.

Furthermore, seniors can involve family members in

decisions regarding the distribution of digital assets in their estate plans. By openly discussing their intentions and involving family members in the decision-making process, seniors can ensure that their digital assets align with family values and objectives, while also offering a unique opportunity for older people to strengthen intergenerational relationships through shared financial planning. By involving family members in discussions and decisions, seniors foster a sense of collaboration, trust, and shared responsibility. This shared experience enhances intergenerational relationships, facilitates mutual understanding, and strengthens family bonds for the long term.

Conclusion

Cryptocurrencies provide senior citizens with a platform to encourage family involvement in financial planning discussions and decisions. By fostering transparency, education, and joint decision-making, seniors can involve family members in cryptocurrency-related matters, ensuring a holistic approach to financial planning. Through inclusive financial training, executor and successor preparation, legacy planning, and intergenerational collaboration, seniors strengthen family relationships and pass on valuable knowledge and skills. Cryptocurrencies serve as a catalyst for family engagement, promoting transparency, shared responsibility, and a sense of unity in managing digital assets and preparing for the future.

Chapter Thirteen

Understanding the Benefits of Retiring with Cryptocurrency

As traditional retirement investment options face challenges, cryptocurrencies offer unique advantages that make them increasingly attractive for retirement portfolios. Inasmuch as it has advantages as a digital asset, cryptocurrency can be utilized effectively in retirement planning to enhance financial security and growth.

Let's start with diversification, as an example.

Diversification is a critical aspect of retirement planning, aimed at reducing risk and maximizing returns. As retirees seek to build a secure and sustainable financial future, the inclusion of cryptocurrency as part of a diversified portfolio can offer unique advantages.

Given as it can serve as a valuable asset within a diversified investment approach, cryptocurrency offers reduced correlation with traditional assets, potential for higher returns, and hedging opportunities. By including cryptocurrency in a retirement portfolio, retirees can access global liquidity, innovative technologies, and potential capital appreciation.

Furthermore, as cryptocurrencies operate on a decentralized network, they allow retirees to access their assets from anywhere in the world with an internet connection. Unlike traditional securities that may be subject to geographic restrictions or limited trading hours, cryptocurrencies enable retirees to engage in transactions 24/7, providing unparalleled accessibility to their investments.

There are also no middlemen and no transaction costs. Which means retirees get to keep more of their wealth.

This takes on increasing importance as the world seems to be heading toward more economic uncertainty and inflation is eating away at people's savings.

Their decentralized nature makes cryptocurrencies resistant to government manipulation and inflationary practices associated with fiat currencies. As a result, individuals can preserve their wealth by holding cryptocurrencies that are not subject to the same inflationary pressures as the traditional money within nation-states .

One case study that presents itself is that of Venezuela. The people there experienced severe hyperinflation, with the bolivar depreciating rapidly. During this period, many Venezuelans turned to Bitcoin as a store of value and a means to preserve their wealth. Bitcoin's decentralized nature and limited supply provided individuals with an alternative to the rapidly depreciating bolivar. While the country faced economic turmoil, those who had diversified their holdings into Bitcoin were able to maintain relative value and protect their wealth.

Likewise consider Cyprus. In 2013, Cyprus faced a severe financial crisis, leading to restrictions on banking transactions and the imposition of capital controls. During this period, Bitcoin gained attention as a way for Cypriots to move their wealth outside the traditional banking system and preserve their funds. Bitcoin's borderless and decentralized nature allowed individuals to transfer and store wealth without being subject to restrictions imposed by the government.

As the Western banking grid is experiencing distress, there is increasing talk about "bail-ins". Unlike a traditional bail-out, a bail-*in* allows a failing commercial bank to legally seize their depositors' savings.

In the United States, the FDIC has quietly changed its rules recently, so that, when a bank fails, depositors are the last in line to get paid back (after all other creditors are compensated). And not all of their savings are insured. It only covers up to $250,000.

By understanding the fundamentals of cryptocurrency, recognizing its advantages for retirement planning, and implementing effective strategies, individuals can harness the potential of this digital asset class to enhance their financial security and growth in retirement. However, it is crucial to approach cryptocurrency investments with caution, seeking professional advice, and staying informed about the ever-evolving regulatory and market landscapes.

CRYPTOCURRENCY FOR SENIORS

As individuals adapt to the changing landscape of retirement planning, cryptocurrencies present a compelling avenue for long-term financial well-being.

Potential Benefits of Retiring with Cryptocurrency

Nigeria affords an example of what happens when ATMs shut down and people are denied access to their own money. In an articleentitled "Riots Erupt in Nigerian Cities as Bank Policy Leads to Scarcity of Cash,"we read, "Banks have limited access to cash for withdrawals because of a scarcity of the new notes, and some businesses refuse to accept old naira, causing huge queues, angering customers and disrupting businesses."

Another article from Firstpost.com asked, "Did China Roll Out Tanks to Prevent People from Withdrawing Money from Banks?"

In it, we read, "For the unversed, China's Henan province has been for the past several weeks witnessing clashes between police and depositors with the latter saying they have been prevented from withdrawing their savings from banks since April this year."

According to *USA Today*,similar things are happening in the West, with the article recounting, "Greeks lined up Monday at ATMs to withdraw no more than $66 — the daily maximum allowed under strict new limits of a financial crisis that closed the nation's banks for a week. Now the limit is 60 euros. Next they'll shut the ATMs down completely. And when we go to get money, they'll give us drachmas," said YiorgosAggelopoulos, 67, a former military officer, referring to Greece's currency before it adopted the euro in 2001."

Likewise, we learn from a 2023 article by *The Guardian*, "Commonwealth Bank Scraps Cash Withdrawals and Deposits at Many Branches Across Australia".

All of these examples highlight the importance of savers to have access to their own money *outside of the traditional banking system*.

With their decentralized nature, cryptographic security, and borderless transaction capabilities, cryptocurrencies empower individuals with greater control over their assets.

And speaking of "borderless," this takes us to another topic . . .

Retirees today are increasingly exploring the option of relocating to different countries to make the most of their retirement savings. This trend is driven by various factors, including the desire for a higher quality of life, lower cost of living, favorable tax regimes, and access to more cost-effective healthcare.

Some additional factors that make this an attractive option are better climate and natural environments, access to more affordable housing, lower crime rates, and so forth.

The trend of retirees relocating to different countries to optimize their retirement savings reflects a desire for superior living conditions, favorable financial circumstances, and access to affordable medical treatments. By considering cost of living, tax regimes, healthcare provisions, and cultural experiences, retirees can identify destinations that align with their preferences and financial goals.

But to be able to take advantage of this option it is critical to have the liquidity and access to one's own funds that cryptocurrency makes possible.

Factors to Consider When Choosing a Retirement Destination

In an article by *Global Citizen Solutions*, we read, "According to a study released by International Living in January 2023, Americans are moving abroad to pursue healthier and happier lives, spend less money, and maximize their retirement goals that they wouldn't ordinarily achieve in their home country."

American retirees, as one example, ranked the factors shaping their decision, as the following.

- Housing
- Benefits and low-cost perks
- Visas and residence ease
- Cost of living
- Cultural assimilation and entertainment
- Quality and accessibility of healthcare
- Development
- Climate
- Government Stability

- Opportunity to semi-retire

Some of their top choices for a retirement destination were Portugal, Mexico, Panama, Ecuador, Costa Rica, Spain, Greece, France, Italy and Thailand.

Portugal, for instance, appears on the best-cost-of-living list for retirees, as well as the top ten countries that are "crypto-friendly". That list runs as follows:

- Malta
- Canada
- Slovenia
- The Netherlands
- Portugal
- Germany
- Luxembourg
- Estonia
- Singapore
- Switzerland

El Salvador, as we mentioned earlier, also made the news in 2021 by declaring Bitcoin to be "legal tender" in their jurisdiction. As did the Central African Republic. (Several additional countries are on the verge of accepting it, as well, including Saint Kitts and Nevis, Ukraine, Paraguay, Venezuela, with Colorado in the U.S. being the first state in America to accept Bitcoin as legal tender.)

Cryptocurrency has emerged as a global phenomenon that impacts retirement planning decisions worldwide. While factors such as the cost of living, tax regulations, and economic stability vary across countries, the increasing adoption of cryptocurrencies introduces new considerations for individuals preparing for their retirement.

Conclusion

Cryptocurrency's impact on retirement planning is influenced by factors such as the cost of living, tax regulations, and economic stability, which vary across countries. The cost of living directly affects retirement savings and necessitates adjustments in income planning. Tax regulations pose unique challenges and require individuals to understand compliance obligations and seek tax-efficient strategies. Economic stability considerations encompass inflation rates, currency stability, and geopolitical risks, which impact long-term financial security. Understanding country-specific dynamics is crucial, as developed and developing countries differ in their regulatory frameworks, adoption rates, and economic conditions. Real-life examples highlight the potential and challenges of utilizing cryptocurrencies for retirement planning in diverse contexts. By considering the influence of cost of living, tax regulations, and economic stability, individuals can navigate cryptocurrency's potential for global retirement security and make informed decisions to optimize their financial well-being.

Chapter Fourteen
Concluding Remarks

The future of cryptocurrencies holds immense potential to transform retirement planning and shape the experiences of senior citizens. As blockchain technology matures (along with the population), cryptocurrencies will provide enhanced investment opportunities, financial inclusion, and autonomy for retirees. However, challenges such as market volatility, regulatory complexities, and cybersecurity threats must be addressed to ensure the safe and sustainable integration of cryptocurrencies into retirement strategies. Educating the aging population, fostering financial literacy, and promoting responsible investment practices will be vital in harnessing the potential benefits and navigating the evolving landscape. By embracing the future possibilities of cryptocurrencies, individuals in retirement can enhance their financial security, access new income solutions, and actively participate in the digital economy, fostering a more inclusive and empowered retirement experience for all.

To recap some of the basic concepts, let's start with wealth-appreciation using cryptocurrencies.

This calls for utilizing strategies and opportunities within the cryptocurrency ecosystem to maximize the value of your digital assets. Here are some ways to appreciate wealth using cryptocurrency. Some of the things to consider are:

CRYPTOCURRENCY FOR SENIORS

1. Long-Term Investment: Holding onto cryptocurrencies with strong potential for growth can lead to appreciation over time. Conduct thorough research, analyze market trends, and identify projects with solid fundamentals before making long-term investment decisions.

2. Dollar-Cost Averaging (DCA): DCA involves regularly investing a fixed amount of money into cryptocurrencies at predetermined intervals, regardless of the asset's price. This strategy allows you to mitigate the impact of short-term market volatility and potentially accumulate more tokens over time.

3. Staking and Yield Farming: Some cryptocurrencies offer staking and yield farming opportunities, allowing you to lock up your holdings in exchange for earning additional tokens or interest. By participating in these programs, you can generate passive income and appreciate your wealth through token rewards or increased asset value.

4. Participating in Initial Coin Offerings (ICOs) and Token Sales: ICOs and token sales provide early-stage investment opportunities in promising blockchain projects. Participating in these events can allow you to acquire tokens at discounted prices, potentially leading to appreciation if the project succeeds.

5. Participating in Decentralized Finance (DeFi): DeFi platforms offer various financial services, including lending, borrowing, and liquidity provision. By utilizing DeFi protocols, you can earn interest, lending fees, or liquidity provider rewards, enabling your cryptocurrency holdings to appreciate.

6. Trading and Arbitrage: Active trading involves buying and selling cryptocurrencies to take advantage of price fluctuations. Trading strategies, such as swing trading or arbitrage, can potentially yield profits and help grow your cryptocurrency wealth.

7. Diversification: Spreading your investments across different cryptocurrencies and sectors can help mitigate risks and capture opportunities for appreciation. By diversifying your holdings, you increase the likelihood of benefiting from the growth of multiple assets.

8. Investing in Blockchain Technology and Infrastructure: Besides investing directly in cryptocurrencies, you can also consider investing in blockchain-focused companies, infrastructure providers, or funds. These investments provide exposure to the broader blockchain industry and its potential for growth.

9. Education and Research: Continuously expanding your knowledge about cryptocurrencies, blockchain technology, and

market trends can help you make informed investment decisions. Stay updated with news, industry developments, and project updates to identify opportunities for wealth appreciation.

10. Professional Advice and Guidance: Seek advice from financial professionals or experts in the cryptocurrency field to gain insights and guidance tailored to your financial goals. They can provide personalized strategies and help you navigate the complexities of the cryptocurrency market.

Secondly, let's summarize the tax implications.

Cryptocurrencies, such as Bitcoin and Ethereum, are subject to tax regulations and reporting obligations. There are several considerations retirees should take into account regarding tax obligations and regulatory compliance when incorporating cryptocurrencies into their retirement strategy.

1. Is cryptocurrency in the region you're retiring to treated as legal tender, or is it classified as property?

2. Is there a capital gains tax levied against transactions in your jurisdiction? (Malta, Switzerland, Belarus, Germany and the Cayman Islands don't impose a capital gains tax on cryptocurrency.) In the United States, by contrast, this is not true. The IRS, moreover, expects taxpayers to report cryptocurrency transactions, including sales, exchanges, and mining income. They provide

Form 8949 for reporting capital gains and losses from cryptocurrency transactions.

3. Are you up to snuff on such reporting and compliance?

4. Have you sought professional advice from knowledgeable tax experts?

5. Have you looked into international tax considerations if you're preparing to retire abroad?

Now let's conclude with some final remarks about the changing nature of the world.

The world is experiencing a significant demographic shift, with populations across the globe growing older. This phenomenon, driven by factors such as declining birth rates and increased life expectancy, has profound implications for society and the economy.

The Industrial Revolution, which in the West started in the 18th Century, brought about significant social and economic changes, including urbanization and the transformation of traditional agrarian societies into industrialized ones. This shift had a profound impact on family dynamics and fertility patterns, leading to a decrease in the number of children people had as they moved into cities.

Much of the world now is experiencing this process as industrialization catches up to them, with a massive tidal wave of people in India, for example, moving from the countryside to crowded cities. China, too—as it industrializes—is seeing birthrates plummet.

This phenomenon, commonly referred to as the "low fertility trap," has been observed in many industrialized nations but has become particularly pronounced in China due to its unique socio-economic and policy factors. The plummeting birthrates in China can be attributed to several key factors, such as urbanization, the rising cost of child-rearing, the country's disastrous one-child policy from 1979 to 2015, and changing gender roles as more women leave the home and go to the factory.

Declining birth-rates and increased access to healthcare are two factors that have shaped a transformational social change, where (as of 2020) there were more retirees than babies being born. Two great books on this phenomenon are *The Demographic Cliff* by Harry Dent and *The Great Demographic Reversal* by Charles Goodhart.

In both volumes, the authors discuss how aging populations in Europe, North America, China and Japan will reshape the world and alter economic buying-patterns. According to these experts, consumer goods (like real estate and automobiles) will see declines as services take center stage (driven by retirees purchasing vacation packages, engaging in more tourism and sight-seeing or receiving healthcare).

Cryptocurrencies have the potential to significantly aid a service-based economy by streamlining payment processes, facilitating global accessibility, reducing transaction costs, enhancing security and privacy, encouraging microtransactions, and fostering decentralized service marketplaces.

Seniors, the world is your oyster! Everything is shaping up to accommodate *you*.

You have conveniences that your parents and grandparents could never have dreamed of. Such as on-demand services, including grocery delivery, meal kits, home maintenance, and transportation services, catering to seniors' convenience and mobility needs. You have Telehealth platforms and remote care services that enable you to access healthcare professionals and receive medical consultations from the comfort of your home.

And should you want to leave that home, you have access to sight-seeing and tourism opportunities that would have been very cost-prohibitive to previous generations.

Likewise, smartphones, tablets, and wearable devices provide opportunities for seamless communication, access to information, and health monitoring, empowering seniors to stay connected and informed.

But, lastly, you have cryptocurrency, which offers you unprecedented economic autonomy, a store of value in a time of eroding fiat currencies, and greater liquidity and access to your own funds as most traditional banks are closing down ATMs and restricting depositors' access to their money.

The emerging world of technology (fueled by the service-based economy) presents transformative possibilities for senior citizens, addressing their specific needs and enhancing their quality of life. From accessible technology interfaces to personalized services, social connections, and supportive care technologies, the integration of technology and service offerings is tailormade to accommodate seniors' preferences, promoting their independence, engagement, and well-being. By embracing these advancements, society can unlock the full potential of senior citizens, fostering an inclusive and age-friendly environment that benefits individuals and society as a whole.

Lastly, here is a list of cryptocurrency resources that can help you stay informed, learn, and engage with the crypto world:

1. Cryptocurrency Exchanges:
   - Coinbase
   - Binance
   - Kraken
   - Gemini
   - Bitstamp

2. Cryptocurrency News Websites:
   - CoinDesk
   - CoinMarketCap
   - Cointelegraph
   - Decrypt
   - Bitcoin.com

3. Cryptocurrency Wallets:
   - Ledger
   - Trezor
   - MetaMask

- Exodus
- MyEtherWallet
4. Cryptocurrency Forums and Communities:
   - BitcoinTalk
   - Reddit (r/Cryptocurrency and specific cryptocurrency subreddits)
   - Telegram (various cryptocurrency-related channels and groups)
5. Cryptocurrency Research and Analytics:
   - CoinGecko
   - CoinMarketCap
   - Messari
   - CoinStats
   - IntoTheBlock
6. Cryptocurrency Education and Learning Platforms:
   - Coinbase Learn
   - Binance Academy
   - CoinMarketCap Earn
   - CryptoCompare
   - Udemy (various cryptocurrency-related courses)
7. Cryptocurrency Social Media Influencers and YouTube Channels:
   - Andreas Antonopoulos
   - Ivan on Tech

- Crypto Daily
- The Modern Investor
- Crypto Kirby

8. Cryptocurrency Podcasts:
   - The Pomp Podcast
   - Unchained by Laura Shin
   - Epicenter
   - Off The Chain
   - The Bad Crypto Podcast

9. Cryptocurrency Research Papers and Whitepapers:
   - Bitcoin: A Peer-to-Peer Electronic Cash System by Satoshi Nakamoto
   - Ethereum Whitepaper by VitalikButerin
   - Ripple Consensus Algorithm Whitepaper
   - Cardano Ouroboros Whitepaper
   - Polkadot Whitepaper

10. Regulatory and Legal Resources:
    - The U.S. Securities and Exchange Commission (SEC) website
    - Financial Action Task Force (FATF) guidelines on cryptocurrencies
    - European Securities and Markets Authority (ESMA) publications on cryptocurrencies
    - Local regulatory bodies specific to your country